John Sherren Brewer

The endowments and establishment of the Church of England

John Sherren Brewer

The endowments and establishment of the Church of England

ISBN/EAN: 9783337261986

Printed in Europe, USA, Canada, Australia, Japan

Cover: Foto ©Lupo / pixelio.de

More available books at **www.hansebooks.com**

THE ENDOWMENTS AND ESTABLISHMENT

OF THE

CHURCH OF ENGLAND.

BY THE LATE J. S. BREWER, M.A.

PREACHER AT THE ROLLS, HONORARY FELLOW OF QUEEN'S COLLEGE, OXFORD,
AND PROFESSOR OF MODERN HISTORY AND LITERATURE
AT KING'S COLLEGE, LONDON.

SECOND EDITION REVISED.

EDITED

BY LEWIS T. DIBDIN, M.A.

OF LINCOLN'S INN, BARRISTER-AT-LAW.

LONDON:
JOHN MURRAY: ALBEMARLE STREET,
1885.

Oxford
Printed by HORACE HART, Printer to the University

SUMMARY.

PART I.

Endowments.

AUTHOR'S PREFACE.—First Part shews that Tithes and Endowments held by the Church were not derived from the nation but individuals.—Second Part shews that Establishment brought no accession of wealth or honour to the Church, but was the control of the Church for the benefit of the nation. — Study of history confirms these statements.—Threefold negative proof. — Questions involved indispensable to national well-being.—Individual right to property, central and social influence of the Church, relation of both to the Crown.—English Constitution formed out of these three principles . . . . 9—12

CHAPTER I.—Dissent free and unendowed.—The Church under control with endowments.—Claim of Dissent that the Church should be free and despoiled.—Church endowments derived from individual benefactors. — Establishment intended to benefit the State . . . . 13—21

CHAPTER II.—Tithes.—Jewish Tithes.—Tithes in the Primitive Church.—St. Augustine on Tithes.—Christianity centred in cities. — Persecution and War scattered Christians and spread Christianity . 22—29

CHAPTER III.—Introduction of Christianity into Britain. —St. Augustine's Mission.—Remains of Roman Art in Kent.—Relics of Christianity.—The Monks Laymen.—Numerous Converts.—Gregory's directions for the disposal of Church offerings.—Two distinct classes,

Monastic and Parochial.—Tithes offered and divided at the Mother Church of the diocese.—As Christianity spread the obligation of Tithes admitted by converts.—Dioceses divided into parishes.—Parochial Clergy required.—Monks not available.—Married Clergy Anglo-Saxons.—Inferior in learning &c. to the Monks.—Kings and Nobles enter the cloister.—Privileges of Monks.—Rapid increase in wealth.—Rage for a monastic life.—Danish Invasion.—Destruction of the Monasteries . . . 30—48

CHAPTER IV.—Christianity maintained by the Bishops and Parochial Clergy.—Clergy driven into the country.—Rise in public estimation.—Promoted to high offices in the Church.—Bishops being Monks at first had little need of their share of the Tithes.—Later lived on the estates attached to their sees by Regal or Noble Donors.—Ethelwulf's grant of Tithes, 855.—Extent of application doubtful.—Present Tithes not derived from this.—Duty of payment of Tithes insisted on from that date.—Bishops resigned their share of Tithes.—Tithes settled on parochial Churches.—But irregularly paid.—Burial Fees more valuable than Tithes.—Burial in City Churches forbidden.—Disposition of Tithes different in different districts.—Numbers of Parish Priests in various counties 49—66

CHAPTER V.—Want of National Unity among the Anglo-Saxons.—Norman Conquest.—State of the Church.—Parochial Clergy removed by Edgar from offices of honour.—Ignorance of rural Clergy.—Dependent upon small endowments of land, gifts of individuals.—True origin of modern Tithes and Endowments.—Nobility and gentry built and endowed Churches for their tenants.—Churches erected by Bishops not Parish Churches, but Chapels of Ease to the Cathedral.—Founders of Parish Churches retained the Advowson.—Founders permitted by Bishops to pay all their Tithes to the Parish Church instead of the Diocesan Fund.—Norman discipline introduced into Church as well as State.—Social and moral effects of the influence of the Parochial Clergy.—System gradually established.—Tithes often diverted.—Monasticism flourishing.—Churches and Tithes handed over to Monasteries by lay-patrons.—Attractions of Abbeys. —Parishes robbed for their benefit.—Vicars appointed. —Aldynge.—Brinkley.—Chalk.—Fascinations of the Religious Houses.—Parochial Clergy pauperized.— Remonstrances of the Commons . . . 67—102

CHAPTER VI.—Spenser on monastic robbers of Churches. —Dissolution of Monasteries transferred their wealth to the King.—Royal appropriation of the Tithes improperly acquired by the Monasteries.—Church thus deprived of a large part of her original endowments.— Distress followed sacrilege.—Parochial Clergy poorer than ever.—State of benefices in Elizabeth's reign.— In Charles I's.—Speech of Sir Benjamin Rudyer.— Queen Anne's Bounty.—Wretched state of parsonages in the 18th century.—Archdeacon Eachard on clerical poverty.—Valuable results to the people of the influence of the Clergy.—The nation has done nothing in return for the Clergy.—The Church established by Henry VIII received no wealth but lost much.— Vivid description of abuses by a contemporary author. —Edward VI.—Elizabeth.—James I.—Charles I.— Restoration of the First Fruits and Tenths by Queen Anne in the Bounty Fund.—Improvement of clerical incomes owing to individual and voluntary contributions. — Benefactions of Drs. Juxon, Sheldon, Warner, Thorndike, Barrow, Gunning, Morley, and Archbishop Sancroft.—Summary of argument; what the Church owes the State . . . 103—125

CHAPTER VII.—Endowments of the Church rest on longer prescription and stronger sanction than other property.—Are well and justly used.—Arguments for disendowment devoid of prudence as well as justice.—If the Nation had endowed the Church it would have no right to resume its gift, unless its retention by the Church were notoriously injurious to the State.—Danger of interference with property   126—133

CHAPTER VIII. — Tithes originally belonged to the Bishop.—Quadripartite Division of Tithes usual in England. — Roman usage. — Gradual growth of Churches and Parishes.—First notice of them in 8th century.—Parish Churches supported out of Diocesan Fund, to which Tithes were paid.—Usurpations of the laity.—Limits of diocesan parishes.—Duty of repairing the Churches.—Efforts of the laity to avoid payment of Tithes by building Chapels.—Manorial Churches and Lay Patronage   .   .   .   .   .   134—150

EDITOR'S NOTES.—I. No grant of Tithes to a particular parish discovered.—Parson's claim to them by *common right*.—Monasteries, Abbeys, Colleges, &c. by *grant* or *prescription*.—Case of Bishop of Llandaff in 1328.—Of the Prior of Christchurch, 1304.—Origin of Tithes probably Apostolic.—Payment of Tithes inculcated as a Christian Duty in St. Augustine's time.—In the 8th century became part of Church Law.—The Conquest gave an impetus to the Tithe system.—Appropriation of Tithes.—Parochial right to Tithes established in the 13th century   .   .   .   151—156

II. Slender evidence as to the tripartite or quadripartite division of Tithes in England.—Alleged law of Ethelred, 1013, probably inoperative. — Selden's view.—Clergy not bound to support the poor and repair the Churches out of Tithe.—Tripartite division if it ever prevailed died out before the custom of tithe-paying crystallized into a legal right   .   .   .   156, 157

PART II.

Establishment.

AUTHOR'S PREFACE.—Various Theories of Establishment. —Henry VIII's Establishment.— Royal Supremacy substituted for Papal Supremacy.—Advantages to the Church. — Disendowment, Confiscation. — Different positions of English and Irish Church.—Disendowment difficult.—Consequently Disestablishment improbable . . . . 161—166

CHAPTER I.— Tithes not national property. — Church ministers to the Nation gratuitously.—Endowment does not imply Establishment.—Wesleyans, Independents, Roman Catholics possess endowments.—Establishment and Endowment totally different.—Notion that the property of the Roman Catholic Church was transferred by Henry VIII to a new Protestant Church without foundation.—What is Establishment? —Government not wrong to confer privileges on a religious society, if it promote the good of the nation.—The Church, however, gained no privileges when established at the Reformation.—The Bishops were in the Lords before Reformation. — Church property no more protected than Dissenters' property. —Church Courts existed before Reformation   167—181

CHAPTER II.—Several meanings of the word "establish." —The Royal Supremacy was new at the Reformation.—It consisted in the right to appoint Bishops.— To assemble and dissolve Convocation, limit its prerogatives, and refer all ecclesiastical causes to himself as final authority.—The Church was not brought into being by Henry VIII.—Henry VIII made no such claim.—Church not weak but strong before Henry VIII.

—Establishment a term applied to the novel relations between Church and State brought about by Henry VIII and Elizabeth.—Reformers never professed to erect the Church on a new foundation.—But claimed to free it from Foreign Jurisdiction.—No new Creeds.—Henry VIII claimed no spiritual function.—Henry's letter to Convocation of York.—Freedom of the Church from Papal Supremacy enabled it to reform itself.—Some see no advantage in substituting the King's authority for the Pope's.—Facts prove that the Church has not suffered by it.—Answer to objection that practically the Royal Supremacy is exercised by Parliament.—Regulated liberty better than liberty subject at any time to interference.—Church too important to escape State Control in some form.—Supremacy of the King not inconsistent with his character as a layman.—He is a *mixta persona*.—Hooker's view on this point . . . . 182—200

CHAPTER III.—Supremacy must be lodged somewhere.—With the Clergy as in the Church of Rome.—The Laity as among Dissenters.—With the King over both, as in the Church of England.—Last plan wisest.—Royal Supremacy equivalent to Establishment. — Church thereby becomes National.—Hooker's theory that the Church and the Nation are one.—If Dissenters refuse to avail themselves of their rights in the Church they have no right to deprive others of theirs.—Dissenters foolish to wish for disestablishment, which, apart from disendowment, would strengthen the position of the Church.—Establishment favourable to moderation.—Requires fixed forms of faith.—Church cannot make new Creeds, Nation cannot alter the Creeds.—No hardship to the Church to be unable to alter her Creed.—If Clergy and Laity differ as to the faith and teaching of the Church an independent judge must decide.—Fixed rule of faith in the Prayer Book.—

Establishment secures the respective rights of Church and Nation, and a permanent standard of faith   201—222

CHAPTER IV.—Establishment benefits the Nation more than the Church.—Advantages of Establishment to the State enumerated.—The State never helps the Church financially. — Disestablishment pure and simple means the complete independence of the Clergy of lay control.—Establishment not unfavourable to spiritual advancement.—No religious faith without dogma.—The true meaning of dogma.—The Church must teach and guide, therefore must insist on Creeds. —Uniformity of faith desirable.—We have religious liberty.—Nothing to say to those who wish to get rid of Christianity altogether.—Believers in "development" who apply scientific processes to Christianity in error.—Development does not affect present obligations.—Christian theory of Development much more startling than Darwin's.—What has been and what will be does not affect present duty.—Some admit we are bound to receive Christianity, but not the Church view of it.—No one compelled to be a Churchman, but if he choose to remain so should be bound by the laws of the Church.—Dissenters in the same position. —The will of any Society must overrule the individual wills of its members.—Dissenters' liberty more apparent than real, ministers amenable to their congregations.—Summary of the chapter under five heads.—The real question not whether Establishment abridges the liberty of the Church, but whether the abridgment is beyond what justice and expediency require   223—257

CHAPTER V.—Establishment secures a new right and title in the Church to the laity.—The Church of England not a denomination.—All Englishmen concerned in it, whether they use it or not.—Church and

State before the Reformation two separate Societies.—Bad effects of separation.—Interest of the Laity in the Reformed Church.—Influence of the Laity good for the Clergy.—Friends of the Church numerous.—General good effect of the present relations of Church and State.—Church always on the side of order.—Position of the Clergy incomprehensible to foreigners.—No wise patriot would tamper with the union between Church and State which has been so successful.—Great services of the Church.—Deserves something better than disendowment.—Disestablishment without Disendowment would restore the *status quo* before the Reformation, minus the Papal Supremacy.—Bishops in the House of Lords a separate question.—Disendowment raises the question how to apply the endowments taken from the Church.—Can they be used more advantageously to the nation than now? . . . . 258—278

CHAPTER VI.—"Established" used in different senses: (1) mere existence, (2) existing and generally accepted, (3) legalized.—None of these definitions apply to the "Established" Church.—Objections to Establishment twofold.—Unjust to the Church because it is prevented improving.—Unjust to Dissenters because it confers honours, emoluments, and authority on the Church but not on them.—Honours.—Seats of the Bishops in the Lords not a part of Establishment.—Emoluments, Tithes, and Endowments, not given by the State at all.—No part of Establishment.—Authority.—Power of the Ecclesiastical Courts to enforce its decrees.—This only binds Churchmen.—In no way interferes with Dissenters.—Establishment means control of Church by State through the Royal Supremacy dating from the Reformation.—Obvious that honours, power, or riches enjoyed by the Church before Establishment cannot be part of Establishment . . . . 279—286

EDITOR'S NOTES.—I. Establishment considered as a *state* as well as an *act.*—Disestablishment would not leave the Church as the Reformation found her.— Coercive Jurisdiction.—Establishment the complex resultant of all the mutual dealings of Church and State, different in different countries.—Disestablishment the fundamental modification of the relations between Church and State so as to reverse resultant. —Mutual Relations of Church and State. A. The Authority exercised by the State over the Church, i. e. Royal Supremacy.—Which consists of: (1) Convocation cannot meet or act without leave of the Crown; (2) Appointment of Archbishops and Bishops; (3) Visitatorial Power; (4) Appeal to the Crown from Ecclesiastical Courts; (5) The Church cannot alter Liturgy, &c. without sanction of the State; (6) Power of the State to mould and modify the machinery for Church discipline.—B. The Privileges enjoyed by the Church, which the State can withhold: (1) Right to exercise Spiritual Jurisdiction; (2) Coercive Jurisdiction; (3) Coronation of the Sovereign by a Bishop or Archbishop; (4) The Sovereign must be a Churchman, and swears to protect the Church; (5) Seats of the Bishops in the House of Lords. All these privileges belonged to the Church before the Reformation . . 287—299

II. *Mixta Persona* theory based on consecration at the Coronation.—Little noticed by English Church writers at or since the Reformation.—Hooker.—Mr. Maskell. —Dr. Stubbs.—Nothing to do with the Royal Supremacy in the Church of England . . 299—301

EDITOR'S PREFACE TO THE SECOND EDITION.

In issuing a new edition of this work very few words of preface will be sufficient. All who know the book will recognise the importance of not letting it remain out of print. Its value as a permanent contribution to the historical literature of the Church of England is undeniable; but in order that it might continue to occupy its proper position in that respect it seemed desirable that some alterations should be made. My principal anxiety has been that the revision should be thorough, and yet the alterations as slight as possible. The little that Mr. Brewer has left to us of his own writing is too valuable to be diminished by needless excision. Accordingly all that has been done is to omit references to individuals and to passing events, and to cut out a few sentences here and there which, in the light of what has happened since Mr. Brewer wrote, seemed out of place. So far as the text is concerned there have been no important omissions, no additions, and only a few obvious emendations. Mr. Brewer's notes have been dealt with in the same manner as the text.

I have ventured to add a few notes, especially two of greater length than the rest—one on the origin of the legal right to Tithes, and the other on the nature of Establishment as an existing institution. I have done so with considerable hesitation, in the hope of assisting the reader to grasp the Author's arguments thoroughly and completely, and to perceive exactly the ground those arguments are intended to cover. Few writers have combined so successfully as Mr. Brewer a glowing style, full of life and interest, with sound, solid reasoning. But the very intentness with which he urges his points, and absorbs himself and his readers in the subject, sometimes tends to obscure the limitations which justice to his argument demands. In his own mind he doubtless took them for granted without noticing that they had not been stated.

But for the exertions of Dr. Wace the Principal of King's College, Mr. Brewer's book would have remained out of print. My share in the work was undertaken at his invitation, and I have been constantly indebted to his knowledge and experience in its progress. I very heartily thank him for his help.

I desire also gratefully to acknowledge the valuable aid I have received from the Bishop of Chester. His Lordship has allowed me to consult him on several points in Part I on Endowments as to which I was in doubt, and by his ready kindness has helped me through more than one difficulty. L. T. D.

6, Stone Buildings, Lincoln's Inn,
Sept. 4, 1885.

CONTENTS.

PART I.

	PAGE
AUTHOR'S PREFACE TO PART I	9

CHAPTER I.
The Question stated 13

CHAPTER II.
The Earliest Forms of Endowments . . . 22

CHAPTER III.
How the Christian Religion was taught, and its Ministers maintained, when Augustine came into England 30

CHAPTER IV.
Commencement of Parochial Churches . . 49

CHAPTER V.
The Origin and History of the Present Tithes and Endowments of the Church of England 67

CHAPTER VI.
Endowments at the Reformation and since . 103

CHAPTER VII.
Conclusion 126

CHAPTER VIII.
Supplementary: Further Account of the Origin of Parochial Endowments 134

Editor's Notes 151

PART II.

	PAGE
Author's Preface to Part II	161

CHAPTER I.
Erroneous Notions Respecting Establishment . 167

CHAPTER II.
Establishment, what it is and in what it consists 182

CHAPTER III.
The Necessity of Establishment 201

CHAPTER IV.
Objections to Establishment considered and answered 223

CHAPTER V.
The Advantages of Establishment . . . 258

CHAPTER VI.
Supplementary: Meaning of the word "Established" 279

Editor's Notes 287

Index 303

ENDOWMENTS AND ESTABLISHMENT.

Part I.

THE ORIGIN AND HISTORY OF TITHES AND ENDOWMENTS.

AUTHOR'S PREFACE TO PART I.

THE nature and purpose of this little volume may be explained in a very few words.

In the First Part of it I have shown that the Tithes and Endowments held by the Church of England have never been derived from the bounty of the nation, as such, but, like those of any other religious or charitable society, are exclusively due to individual charity and munificence.

In the Second Part I have shown that Establishment brought no accession of honour, wealth, or authority to the Church, but rather the reverse. It was no more than the control of the Church by the State, exercised through the Royal Supremacy, exclusively for the benefit of the nation, and not of the Church.

These two positions are so obvious as to require no great knowledge of English history; for whoever will consider either of them for a few minutes will at once perceive that as Henry VIII. and the Tudor sovereigns, under whom the Church was *established*, in the strict meaning of the word, were anxious to *establish* their authority over it, it was not in the least likely that they would increase its power of resisting their will by increasing its wealth, privileges, authority, or influence.

And, secondly, as the tithes and endowments of the Church of England are not held by it in a corporate capacity, but are severally the endowments of every parish church in England, and as such churches were not built simultaneously but successively, no one general national endowment was possible. If endowments had been provided by the nation, they must have been the result of successive acts, as churches were built; which no one imagines.

And, thirdly, if either of the opposite suppositions were true, as maintained by Mr. Miall and others, some record of them must have been found either in the Statute Book or the ancient Chroniclers; whereas those who uphold them may be fearlessly challenged to produce any evidence whatever from either of these sources in support of their assertions.

Not contenting myself, however, with this negative kind of proof, conclusive as it is, I have in this volume traced the origin and history of Endowment and Establishment, and explained the meaning and intention of both by reference to facts. For these are matters of fact only,—a consideration mainly overlooked, or forgotten, by those who write or talk on these subjects.

The questions involved in them lie at the root of our national life, and have never been totally absent from the minds of Englishmen at any epoch of our history, still less at the advents of great national struggles. By them legislation has been mainly determined and shaped; for they are no more than peculiar phases of the three great principles, upon the true adjustment of which our chief thoughts and energies as a nation have always been concentrated; I mean, the personal and individual rights of property, so dear to the mind of the Anglo-Saxon; the central and social influence of the Church, out of which all modern society has been developed; and the relation of both to the Crown. The true adjustment of these three principles is indispensable to our national life and well-being. The combination of one with the other to the depression of the third; or the undue exaltation of any one of the three, through the power of some great king, pope, or popular leader, has always led the way to great constitutional struggles, ending only when their equilibrium was restored. As each of these influences, and all of them together, are liable to continual change, and have always been operative, even when not prominent or not perceived, it is hard to represent their exact condition at any era, or to determine exactly how far society is influenced by them at any given time. Popes are never so strong as they appear in their canons and councils, nor kings so powerful and arbitrary as they seem in their actions. Custom and prescription, stronger than law, controlled the wills and intentions of both. Usage and precedent overruled the indefinite authority of the great lay lords and secured freedom for their inferiors—a freedom, happily for us, resting not upon law, but upon personal influence, restraint, and custom.

Out of the adjustment of these three principles has grown our constitution in Church and State, and they must always be carefully taken into account in forming a correct judgment on such subjects as are discussed in this volume.

July, 1873.

THE ORIGIN AND HISTORY OF TITHES AND ENDOWMENTS.

CHAPTER I.

THE QUESTION STATED.

In looking at the state of society in England it is impossible not to perceive a great inequality in the religious bodies of which that society is composed. That inequality does not extend merely to differences of faith, worship, discipline, or even of numbers, but to the various degrees of favour and encouragement these bodies are supposed to receive from the State. If a dissenter is anxious to maintain or disseminate his religious opinions, or secure for himself and for others what he believes to be the most appropriate form of worship, he must build a chapel at his own cost, and procure or provide some maintenance for its minister. It matters not what those opinions are, or how diverse that mode of worship may be from that which is generally acceptable to his fellow-men; provided only that he keeps within the letter of the law, and does not offend public morals and public decency, the State will not interfere with him. He may, if he pleases, erect his chapel and maintain a ministry for the propagation of Christianity or the reverse, for the denunciation of creeds and sacraments, or the encouragement of the extremest assertions of Popery. He may accept or deny the authority of Scripture, proclaim or vilify the doctrine of the Trinity: nay, more, the chapel he has built for the dissemination of one set of religious opinions, he may, if he likes, convert to an opposite purpose, or sell, or alienate to secular uses. And as the State will not interfere with his liberty of action in this respect, so neither will it interfere with any mode he may choose to adopt of conducting religious worship, or any ceremonies, or any mode of church government whatsoever, however monstrous, absurd, or ridiculous they may appear to others. He claims the right of private judgment in matters of religion, and the State allows it him unconditionally. He protests against any interference in matters of conscience between himself and his God, and the State admits the protest. He urges that no one man, nor any body of men, can be judge of another man's faith; for to his own Master alone he must stand or fall. And though this tenet, if consistently carried out, would preclude a dissenter from judging of any other man's faith, and therefore denouncing it, however false and erroneous it might be,— and though it would imply no essential difference between a conscientious belief in the truth and a conscientious belief in falsehood,—the State is content. If he preaches the truth the State takes no notice of it, and neither honours nor rewards him for so doing. Also, if he preaches error, destructive to the spiritual welfare of himself and others, it takes no notice. It neither punishes nor prevents him. How can it? For it follows from the very ground on which the dissenter claims unconditional religious liberty, and denies the right of interference with his religious convictions, that the State can neither reward him nor punish him. For that would be, as it were, to constitute itself a judge between him and his God, which the dissenter denies the State is justified in doing. With his freedom, then, to maintain the truth, he is also free to fall into error. With his freedom to proclaim Christianity, he is free also to deny every one of its doctrines. With his freedom to set up a place of worship wherever he likes, he is also free to remove or abandon it at his pleasure. Provided he can find any to listen to him, he may be the most learned or the most ignorant of pastors; the most enlightened or the most superstitious; the most exalting or the most degrading. For as he is free by the laws of the land to erect a chapel when and where he can, and bring a congregation about him, his congregation are equally free, by the same laws, to choose or abandon their pastor at their own pleasure or convenience. If he is influential and powerful, he is in effect supreme over his congregation; if he is friendless and unpopular, they are supreme over him. In fact dissenters and their congregations are purely voluntary associations, rising and falling like other voluntary associations, and left by the State to manage, or even to mismanage, their own affairs, according to their own convictions or caprices.

It is otherwise with the Church of England. Like dissenters, indeed, it has to build churches and find endowments for its ministers. But then, also, it has churches and endowments all over the land, of very ancient date, the exclusive possession of which is guaranteed to the Church by the State. These fabrics and these endowments it cannot alienate, or destroy, or apply to secular uses. So far from being exclusively dependent on itself for pecuniary support, or the means for propagating its teaching, it receives a very large sum in the form of tithes from all the land of England, in a certain state of cultivation. It has other endowments in the shape of glebe-lands; and the exclusive enjoyment of these various emoluments is secured to it by the State, and to the Church exclusively. Its various orders, its forms, its ordinances, its creeds, articles, and professions of faith, are recognized by the State, and cannot be changed without the consent of the State, which is as much interested in maintaining them as the Church itself is. In any internal disputes between clergy and clergy, or between clergy and laity, the State decides, not in conformity with its own laws, but in conformity with the creeds, rubrics, and articles of the Church. Its chief dignitaries are appointed by the State, or by the Crown in behalf of the State. Its bishops sit in the House of Lords, and form part of the legislature of the nation. From these advantages it is supposed that the Church of England derives great social benefits to the prejudice of other religious communities.

And as large bodies of dissenters apparently differ little in their teaching from the main doctrines of the Church of England—excepting only the Roman Catholics (now claimed by the Nonconformists as a portion of themselves), and the Unitarians and Secularists;—and as they have laboured hard and usefully among the neglected classes of the community, the wealth and honours appropriated by the nation exclusively to the Church appear to many a violation of that impartiality which ought to be extended to all. Dissatisfied with the concession of their former demand of perfect liberty of conscience, the dissenters now insist, somewhat inconsistently, that all religious bodies shall become dissenters like themselves. They deny that the State, as such, should have any conscience, or that it has any right to establish any religion according to its conscience, however pure, faultless, or true that religion may be; however much it may be conducive to good government; however great the benefits the nation has received or may receive from it. Every individual of the nation is to believe the truth, and to worship God in conformity with his belief, no man interfering with him; but all men as one body are to have no belief, nor are they to worship according to the best of their belief. In short, the nation must have no religious convictions at all, but treat all faiths alike, or rather regard all with the same indifference, whether, according to its opinion, they contribute to the general welfare of the State or the reverse. This is the position taken up by the dissenters. And therefore they do not claim that their efforts in the cause of religion and morality should be regarded with any favour by the State, but that they should only be tolerated. As they are willing to forego all the advantages of State favour, the Church of England, which does not think so, ought (they contend), in the cause of religious liberty, to be compelled to think as they think. It should be suffered no longer to enjoy those distinctions and that patronage which, in their estimation, it now enjoys. Further, as it possesses considerable endowments, and its ministers are mainly supported by tithes, the dissenters propose that it should hold those endowments no longer; not because the Church does not require them, not because it abuses them, not because it fails to employ them in the propagation and maintenance of religious truth, but because the exclusive possession of them constitutes an invidious distinction between the Church of England and themselves. And, further, it seems unjust that the nation should reserve its wealth and its honours exclusively for one religious body, however great, patriotic, or important that body may be, whilst other religious bodies possess no such advantages, but are exclusively dependent on their own unassisted exertions.

It will be my purpose then, in the following pages, to trace the origin and history of the tithes and endowments of the Church of England. In so doing I shall show by incontestible evidence that these endowments were not given by the nation, as such, at all, at any period of its history, but were the voluntary contributions of individual benefactors. I shall further show that they are precisely of the same nature, and no other, as the charitable funds or the chapels possessed by dissenters. If then justice demands that the Church should be deprived of its endowments, the same justice, to be even-handed, ought to confiscate the chapels and religious funds of dissenters, for both have sprung from the same origin. I shall show also, that as dissenters have exclusively depended on their own exertions, without any aid from the State, the Church has done precisely the same; nay more, that it has suffered more in the alienation, waste and confiscation of its property by the State, than all the dissenting bodies put together. And, finally, I shall show that for the security of its property it enjoys no other legal advantages from the State than what are extended to all classes of dissenters; but rather the reverse; the State taking where it has not given, and reaping where it has not sown.

In the second part of this treatise I propose to explain the true nature, meaning, and purpose of Establishment—a subject as much misunderstood and misrepresented as that of endowments. And I shall make it clear that Establishment, so far from being intended by the State as a mode of doing honour to the Church, was and is mainly designed for the benefit of the State itself and for that of the nation at large.

CHAPTER II.

THE EARLIEST FORMS OF ENDOWMENTS.

THE Jews under the Old Testament paid tithes to the Levite, and every second year a tithe of their goods besides to the poor. The more strict and devout among them did not confine themselves to the letter of the law in this respect, but went farther, some out of real, some from affected piety. It is to this custom that our Lord alluded when He rebuked the Pharisees: "Ye pay tithe of mint and anise and cummin," He says, which the law did not require, "and have omitted the weightier matters of the law, judgment, mercy, and faith;" and He adds, "*these ought ye to have done*, and not to leave the other undone."[1] That is, He fully admits the rightfulness of their conduct in the strict payment of tithes for the maintenance of the Levite and relief of the poor, but He condemns them for thinking that punctiliousness in this respect could atone for weightier omissions. It is this righteousness of the Pharisees to which He

[1] Matt. xxiii. 23.

again refers when He tells His disciples, "Except your righteousness shall exceed the righteousness of the scribes and Pharisees, ye shall in no case enter into the kingdom of heaven."[2]

Now when the Church arose after our Lord's resurrection, and the first Christian community was formed at Jerusalem, Christian converts still paid their tithes and offerings as before, though it was in behalf of a religion which they believed had been superseded, and for the benefit of priests and Levites who were their bitterest persecutors. But in addition to these payments they burthened themselves by contributing to the necessities of the nascent churches, both at Jerusalem and elsewhere. Some, like Barnabas, sold their possessions, and laid the money at the Apostles' feet; that is to say, left it in the power of the Apostles to distribute it as they pleased. "And the multitude of them that believed were of one heart and of one soul: neither said any of them that ought of the things which he possessed was his own; but they had all things common."[3] The practice thus commenced

---

[2] Matt. vi. 20.
[3] Acts iv. 32. Not meaning that they had community of goods; for, if so, St. Paul would not have exhorted Christian congregations to lay up in store on the first day of the week, as God had prospered them (1 Cor. xvi. 2), but rather have

continued; it was not likely, if we consider the accumulating force of Christian tradition, to be changed. The offerings and contributions made by Christians were laid at the feet of the Apostles and of the Apostles' successors, and were distributed by them and according to their appointment, by deacons in the first instance, by priests and deacons afterwards. So matters stood until the taking of Jerusalem. But when the temple was destroyed and the Jews were dispersed, they were released from the obligation of tithes, first-fruits, and oblations, as they are to this day, having neither temple nor priesthood.

Considering the fervour of the first ages of the Church, it is not in the least degree probable that Christians would retain these tithes to their own use. It is in the highest degree probable that they would still dedicate them to God's service. But whatever opinion may be held on that point, it is certain that the liberality of Christians in support of their ministers and their poor was so bountiful as to attract even the

rebuked them for violating the first law of Christian communion. I am inclined to think that these words are little else than an enlargement and illustration of the foregoing: "They had *one* heart and *one* soul;" unlike those sects and divisions by which they were surrounded. In Christ all men feel a *common* interest, all men find a common salvation; for exclusiveness is done away—there is neither Jew nor Greek, bond nor free.

attention of the heathen. It is equally certain that from very early times tithes formed a part of that munificence. "All the faithful in town and country," says Justin Martyr, in the second century, "meet at the Sacrament, and that done, pay their contributions to the common fund; from which the chief minister (the bishop) dispenses what is meet for the sick, the poor, the widow, and the stranger."[4] "Let Christians keep for themselves," says St. Augustine, "as much as is sufficient. Let them keep more than is sufficient. But let us give some part. What part? A tithe. The scribes and the Pharisees paid tithes, for whom Christ had not yet shed His blood."[5]

Such was the custom of paying tithes among Christians: a spontaneous offering at first, afterwards insisted on by the Church as a duty.[6] It is not pretended that tithes were made universally obligatory by any civil decree or imperial constitution. That could not be before the time

[4] Apolog. i. § 67. [5] S. Augustini Opera, v. 654.
[6] Though our Lord enjoined upon His disciples, "Freely ye have received, freely give," this did not prevent St. Paul from insisting on the duty of all men to provide for those who are of the household of faith. "Do ye not know," he says, "that they who minister about holy things live of the sacrifice? and they who wait at the altar are partakers with the altar? *Even so hath the Lord* (that is, Christ Himself) *also ordained*, that they who preach the Gospel should live of the Gospel." (1 Cor. ix. 13.)

of the Emperor Constantine, nor yet till long after. For in every city of the empire, and still more in the rural districts, pagans abounded; and it would not have been just to have compelled them to maintain a religion which they did not embrace, and from which they received no benefit.[7] Nor would the Church have accepted such offerings.[8] *Communicate, communion, having all things in common*, were only different expressions

[7] There would be no analogy, in this instance, between the pagan and the dissenter. For the pagan would have had to pay tithe out of his own property, but the dissenter in paying tithes is discharging an incumbrance which was on his land when he acquired it, and the existence of which was considered in assessing the purchase-money or rent which he was to pay. He is therefore no loser by tithes. He only fulfils a trust he is bound to fulfil: unless it is contended that when a man buys a piece of land with a mortgage or settlement upon it he may honestly repudiate the obligation. [The real losers by payment of tithes in any particular case are the descendants, if there are any, of the original donor who, many centuries ago at the latest, diminished the value of his estate by giving to the Church a tenth of its produce. This diminution has fallen exclusively on the donor and his descendants, whether they have retained possession of their estate or whether they have sold it. In the former case (a very rare one) they have received less profits, in the latter case less purchase money, than they would have received had there been no dedication of tithes.—L.T.D.]

[8] By a canon of the Council of Illiberis (A.D. 277), it is decreed that no offerings shall be received from excommunicated persons. The same restriction would of course apply to idolaters.

THE EARLIEST FORMS OF ENDOWMENTS. 27

of the same idea; all implied an intimate society and union of men bound together in one fellowship and brotherhood of reciprocal benefit. And thus, as we have seen before,[9] all communion, even as far back as the age of the New Testament, implied not only a participation of the body and blood of Christ, but an acknowledgment on the part of all, who were thus brought into one body, of their mutual obligations. As St. Paul expresses it, "Let him that is taught in the word *communicate* unto him that teacheth in all good things."[1] Or, as he elsewhere expresses the same thought, "communicating to the necessity of the saints" where we have translated it, "*distributing* to the necessity of saints;"[2] the alms of the faithful, as Justin Martyr has shown, being collected at the Holy Communion, and distributed by the Apostles and their successors, as every man had need.

As Christianity was gathered up in cities,[3] where there was one Church, under one chief pastor, or bishop (overseer), and there only[4] the

[9] P. 23, n. 3.   [1] Gal. vi. 6.
[2] Rom. xii. 13. [The Revised Version adopts Mr. Brewer's corrected reading. L.T.D.]
[3] And so, it might be thought, our Lord had enjoined, for He says expressly, "When they persecute you in this *city,* flee ye into *another.*" Matt. x. 23.
[4] See Fr. de Berlendis De Oblat., p. 259, Venet. 1743. A most able work.

sacrifice of Christ's mystical body was offered in all its suggestiveness, there also the offerings of the whole Christian congregation were made. There all their tithes were paid, and distributed into four parts, still following in great measure the ancient usage. One part of them was reserved for the bishop, a second part for the clergy who resided with him at the church or cathedral, a third part for its reparation and the necessities of divine service, and a fourth part was bestowed on the poor and the stranger, or upon "hospitality," to use St. Paul's language.[5]

Such then was the practice of the Christian Church, such the form of its ministration and maintenance, when Augustine was sent by Pope Gregory into England to convert our pagan forefathers. But before I conclude this chapter I must advert to one consideration which I think will have occurred to my readers. If there was only one church, and that in a city, what provision was made for the religious instruction of the poor in the country? What resident minister had they to proclaim unto them the glad tidings of the Gospel? Very little I fear it must be said. The bishop indeed sent out his clergy to administer Baptism and teach in the neighbouring villages; but that could not be very far, nor very effectual. For as late as the sixth

[5] [See note, p. 156.]

century the poor country people were still found worshipping the heathen god Apollo, not eighty miles from Rome![6] At the same time it must be remembered that, for many miles round the great cities of the empire, the country people drove their flocks into the suburbs at nightfall for greater security; a precaution all the more indispensable when the Goths and the Huns invaded Italy and filled the country with runaway slaves, robbers, and marauders. And here we see how the wisdom of God brought great good out of evil. For as not only Christianity was gathered up in cities, and all that made Christianity outwardly attractive, but, as in these Roman cities was collected the spoil of the world, so all was dispersed, disseminated, and scattered by the inroads of the barbarians; and like a rich and ripe shock of corn, the seed was shaken out in all directions to take root elsewhere and bear fruit upward. By war, by persecution, priests, bishops, and Christian laymen were compelled to flee and wander "in deserts, and in mountains, and in dens and caves of the earth." So Christianity, debased by the luxury and effeminacy of great and profligate cities, was purified; and the word of the Gospel became known where its tidings had never reached before.

[6] By St. Benedict when he founded his monastery on Monte Cassino.

CHAPTER III.

HOW THE CHRISTIAN RELIGION WAS TAUGHT, AND ITS MINISTERS MAINTAINED, WHEN AUGUSTINE CAME INTO ENGLAND.

IN the minds of the Romans this island was associated with all that was gloomy and terrible. Little known, in consequence of its isolation from the rest of Europe, it was supposed to lie on the utmost verge of the habitable world. Its climate was as strange, abnormal and spectral, as its inhabitants exceeded all others in brutality and ferocity. It was an achievement counted worthy of the greatest general of the age, to have landed on its coasts, and exposed the disciplined valour of the Roman legions to the naked courage and impetuous onsets of its savage inhabitants. And probably it was much more the effect that such an attempt would produce on the imagination of his countrymen, than any material advantage, that induced Cæsar, then

HOW THE CHRISTIAN RELIGION WAS TAUGHT. 31

aiming at the Imperial Crown, to embark on so hazardous an enterprise.

Britannicus (*Conqueror of Britain*) was a title selected by the successors of Cæsar to be stamped upon their medals, as an indication of their prowess. This old feeling of dread had not entirely passed away at the close of the sixth century, when Pope Gregory determined upon sending St. Augustine into England. If the old story may be trusted, he was struck with the large limbs and bright complexions of certain slaves exposed to sale in the great Roman capital. They must have been more than ordinarily conspicuous for their beauty and their stature; for Gregory had often seen hundreds of slaves, in the market at Rome, and never been attracted by the sight before. On inquiry, he found that they were natives of Britain, had come from the province of Deira (Durham), and were pagans, like the rest of their countrymen. In the quaint language of the story, he resolved to make *Angels* of these *Angles;* for such angelic faces, he thought, were fit for the companionship of angels in Heaven.[1]

But how to set about it? He was not per-

[1] The whole story is evidently of Northern origin, as is shown from the names Angli, Ælla, and Deira, on which Gregory descants. It may, however, be substantially true, though coloured with the poetical imagination of the North.

mitted himself to undertake their conversion, and where were Christian Missionaries to be found willing to brave the dangers of so perilous an enterprize? Who were to cross stormy seas and mountains, and preach the Gospel to a race known only to the Romans for their fair hair, their fierce blue eyes, and their untamable ferocity? Even if the Church, habituated to a city life, had been so inclined, it had no missionaries to spare. Its priests, accustomed to the presence of their bishop, living with him in the same cathedral college, never acting without his guidance and advice, were not suited for the task, and in fact had their missionary stations and circuits at home. But Gregory, some years before, had made the acquaintance of a society of men who had withdrawn from the world, especially from a city life, so attractive to their contemporaries, in order to devote themselves to the service of God, and live by the labour of their hands. These were the monks of St. Benedict, destined to exercise an influence so wonderful as almost to change the whole face of the world in a few years, and leave a lasting impression behind them, of which we witness the effects even to this day. It was from this society of men, only then recently established in Italy, that Gregory selected forty missionaries, with

St. Augustine at their head, and sent them into England.

In 597 the new missionaries landed at Thanet, in Kent, where Ethelbert was reigning with Bertha his queen, of the royal race of France. She was a Christian, and for her use the church of St. Martin, near Canterbury, built by the Romans when they inhabited Britain, had been reserved.[2] It was in Kent, about 150 years before, that the Saxons had first established themselves, as a predatory band from the Continent. In this long period of five generations, their ancient faith, uprooted from its native soil, must in their new settlements, so different from the old, have grown feebler, and already have fallen to decay. For Kent was utterly unlike the inextricable forests and boundless plains of the land they had left. It was highly cultivated. It was studded with the remains of Roman art. Roman forts, walls, aqueducts, baths, and churches, met the eye of its barbarous and pagan possessors. Even now, 150 years after the invasion of the Anglo-Saxons, two churches at least existed, in fact, close to the walls of Canterbury and the palace of the sovereign. If that were so, we may infer that these were not

[2] Another church, also built by the Romans, served for the Metropolitan See of Canterbury. Bede, E. H. i. 33.

isolated instances; that the material remnants of another faith and a higher civilization continually met the eyes of our Anglo-Saxon forefathers. Their conquest of the island had been very gradual; generation after generation passed away before they were masters of the whole. It is impossible then that they could have massacred, at a stroke, the whole Celtic population, and have converted the island into a desert. The fact seems to be, that the Romanized Britons, who had lost all nationality and all feeling of independence, only changed masters, and after a few sanguinary but ineffectual struggles, submitted, Christians as they were, to pagans, the civilized to the barbarians. Some fled, others yielded and became the slaves and drudges of the conqueror, doing for him the menial work he would not do for himself, tilling the land whilst he wielded the sword.[3] As the Briton had before submitted to the Roman, and abandoned his national faith and his language, so now with equal flexibility he submitted to the Anglo-Saxon, and with similar results.

[3] "Some, worn out with hunger," says Bede, "submitted to the enemy, and for supplies of food preferred to endure unremitting slavery." E. H. i. 15. This was the fate of the Anglo-Saxons themselves at the Norman Conquest.

It was impossible for the Anglo-Saxon to be exposed to all these influences and not be affected by them. Unknown even to himself a change had been going on favourable to the reception of a better faith, which his forefathers at their first coming had despised, when they saw it exemplified in the debased and denationalized Briton. So God prepared the soil for the seed, and the workman, as we shall presently see, for his labour.

After some natural trepidation of the new missionaries at the perils of their task, and equally natural delay on the part of Ethelbert, the work of conversion went rapidly forward. The people heard them gladly. Multitudes believed and were baptized.

It must be remembered that St. Augustine and his forty companions were monks; that is to say, with the exception of St. Augustine himself and a few others, they were laymen, not ecclesiastics, who had devoted themselves to a life of meditation and prayer, and lived by the labour of their hands. It might have been thought that with so many labourers and so vast a harvest before them, it would have been better had they been dispersed and despatched on different missions. Happily this could not be. They were a society bound together by religious vows, exemplifying in their lives, so far as they understood them, the self-denying ordinances of the earliest Christian communities. Working with their own hands, frugal in their dress and meals, they were independent of other men's charity. It could not be said, nor even thought, that in thus settling in a distant and dangerous country they were actuated by any motives of self-interest. At midnight, in the early morning, again at noon-tide and evening, the poor pagan Anglo-Saxon, as he passed their humble oratory, heard these monks, with their cultivated voices, singing praises unto God. Early in the morning as they rose to their labour, and late in the evening when their labour was ended, their voices floated and fell upon the gale, like the music of unseen angels, to the fancy of the simple Anglo-Saxon peasant, who had never heard anything akin to it before.[4] The Anglo-Saxons were fond of music. To this day psalmody, though far less effective than the psalmody of the monks, has a wonderful influence over English feelings. Then it was as strange as it was ravishing. Again, early in the morning they saw this silent and mysterious fraternity, in their monastic dresses,

[4] "The ploughman at his plough, the harvestman at his task, the vine-dresser with his knife, would each solace his labours with a psalm." St. Jerome.

with composed looks and thoughtful gesture, proceeding two and two to their labours in the fields; there to dig, and ditch, and plough, as if they had been born for no other purpose; to labour like slaves, but how unlike the idle, worthless, and wasteful slaves of their own land! To a simple and unlettered people, how could Christianity recommend itself more effectually, than in the example of this devoted, patient, and mysterious brotherhood? They alone could imitate the works of ancient days. They alone could plant, and build, and teach, as the famous men of old had done. They alone were the exclusive possessors of art, of science, of books, of pictures, and antiquities. They alone knew what was equally good to cure the body and save the soul. The Saxon peasants who came to look upon them were already converted by their eyes, before the truths these missionaries had to tell had reached their ears.

And then these monks were laymen, labourers like themselves. No better fed or clothed than they. What must that religion be which could produce such wonderful effects as these!

Augustine soon found himself surrounded by a large and increasing body of converts, of whom the poor, the sick, and the slave formed no inconsiderable portion. How was he to provide for them? What rules should he adopt for his new society? These are the questions which now engage his attention. He addresses himself to his ancient master, Pope Gregory. "How," he inquires, "are bishops to live with their clergy? What division is to be made of the offerings of the faithful at the altar? By what rules are bishops to be guided?"

After referring his inquirer to St. Paul's Epistles to Timothy, as the clearest exposition of the duties of a bishop, Gregory proceeds to answer the second question. He tells Augustine that it is the practice of the Apostolic See for all offerings made to the Church to be divided into four portions, " one of which is to be reserved for the bishop and his household, that he may exercise hospitality; a second, for his clergy; a third, for the poor; and a fourth, for the repair of the churches."[4]

Then, he continues—and this must be specially observed—" Because you, my brother, brought up under monastic rule, cannot separate yourself from the clergy of the Church of England, which by the instrumentality of God has been lately brought to the knowledge of the faith, you are to follow such a mode of living as was adopted by our fathers in the infancy of the Church, *when none said that ought of the things which he possessed were*

[See note, p. 156.]

his own, but they had all things common.[5] So although Augustine was archbishop, and the head of the Church of England, he was not to forsake the rule and society of his monks, but continue to be their abbot and archbishop at the same time. "But," subjoins the Pope, "if there be any who cannot remain single, let them marry, but arrangements must be made for them elsewhere, and not in the monastery. For we learn by the same Scripture that division was made 'to all men, as every man had need.'[6] Some provision," he continues, "must be set apart for them, and they must be amenable to ecclesiastical rule, living moral lives, and giving diligence to the singing of Psalms. As for those," he continues, "who are living in common (i.e. the monks), I need give no advice about dividing tithes or offerings among them, or hospitality, or works of mercy, since all that is not absolutely necessary for their support is to be distributed in religious and pious works."[7]

If these remarks be carefully considered they will explain many difficulties, and the reader will clearly understand the position, which has been so often misrepresented, of the Church and its clergy in this country before the Conquest.

[5] Acts iv. 32. [6] Acts ii. 45.
[7] Bede, E. H. i. 27, § 59.

It will be seen that there were two bodies, perfectly distinct in their main characteristics, employed from the first in the service of God. Of these one was monastic, the other clerical or parochial; the former confined to the cloister and bound to celibacy, the other married and living in the world. The one gained their livelihood by manual tasks, the other were supported by the tithes and offerings of the faithful. The one consisted of spiritual men only, the other of laymen, in the main; though some of them might be ordained as the wants of their convent required. But though they thus became priests, and administered the sacraments, or heard confession, which the rest of their brethren could not do, they were still essentially monks, bound by the rules of their order, amenable to its discipline, and necessarily resident within the walls of their abbey, except under rare and peculiar circumstances. Of both bodies the archbishop was the superior in the first instance. He ruled his monks, lived amongst them, and ate at their table, practised the same austerities, submitted to the same rigid discipline.[s] The retirement thus afforded him

[s] The two offices were afterwards separated, and the monastery was ruled by a prior, but still the authority of the archbishop or the bishop of the diocese was supreme. Afterwards, through the favour of the Pope, the monasteries

from the pressing cares of his office, often aggravated by grave political duties, was of the utmost value. Their libraries, the only ones that existed, provided him with means of study. Their lives spent in one unceasing round of devotion refreshed his spirit, and furnished an example of peace, order, harmony, and obedience, to which the world without offered a wearisome and noisy contrast. It was in fact a refuge from the storms of life, all the more attractive, because the bishop had no domestic circle, no comforts at home—nothing in fact that could solace, cheer, or amuse him.[9]

But the archbishop, or bishop, was also the chief and head of his diocese, co-extensive at the first with the old divisions of the Heptarchy. That is to say, there was one bishop for the chief or capital town, whose church was its cathedral —the mother church of the whole province. To the altar of this church all offerings were made, all tithes were brought, and divided as Gregory had

contrived to withdraw themselves entirely from the jurisdiction of the bishop, and even forbade him to enter their walls without their consent.

[9] There are repeated instances to be found of priests, nobles, and others, offering land and large sums of money to the religious houses for permission to walk in their gardens, or have a chamber or corrody (that is, a pension or sustentation) within their walls.

enjoined.[1] From this church, as from a common centre, the bishop sent out his clergy to minister to the spiritual wants of the people. At first, and for some interval after the arrival of St. Augustine, there were no parishes, no parish churches, no residence, no endowments for a parochial clergy. There could be none. And as the progress of Christianity was gradual, and the whole of England was divided into independent kingdoms, which received the faith at different periods, there was and there could be no national provision made for the wants of the Church, still less any grand idea of setting up a body to christianize the nation.

As Christianity spread, and as far as it spread, the obligation of maintaining it by tithes and offerings was admitted by Christian converts. It arose from no national enactment, and required none. As the Church grew, the fund for its maintenance grew with it; comparatively small at first, it sufficed for the needs of each diocese; just as the one mother Church and its clergy sufficed for the spiritual wants of the diocesan congregation. The fund increased as the circle spread, but then also arose the necessity of a larger and more effectual spiritual provision. More clergy would be required; and the old method of one *parochia* (one great parish)

[1] [See note, p. 156.]

co-extensive with the diocese, with one supreme pastor and preacher, who should superintend all and all concerns, was no longer sufficient. So dioceses were divided into parishes and the clergy became more dispersed.

Now it will be remembered, as I have said, how attractive these monasteries must have been, not only to the poor, unenlightened Anglo-Saxons themselves, but even to their teachers and rulers. Their immense superiority to all others could not be denied. If religion anywhere put on its most becoming, most attractive, or most commanding aspect, nowhere was it so conspicuous as among the monks. Nowhere else did men seem so completely to realize the most arduous precepts of the Gospel; nowhere was the ideal of Christian brotherhood, or equality, more effectively fulfilled; nowhere had men apparently learned so thoroughly to count all things as dung, so that they might win Christ.

But more than this; these monks had left home and country to serve God, and exemplify their profound belief in the religion they professed in order to teach it to these poor and benighted Anglo-Saxons. Many of them were of noble race, and all of a famous country. Their whole appearance, manners, gestures, speech, and gait, regulated and subdued to a second nature by the strictest discipline, marked them out as superior beings, fitted to guide and to command, and whose commands were obeyed with pleasure. What then could Augustine do? Some that were not in orders he might ordain, and employ them as missionary preachers in the conversion of the Anglo-Saxons. But a large portion of them must still remain as monks to carry on the work of the monastery, and provide by their labour for the support of the rest. Further, they were celibates. Therefore the married clergy, of whom Gregory speaks, who could not be collected into the monastery, but were to be employed elsewhere, must have been such of the natives as embraced the faith, and were willing to enter the ministry. Now as there was no Anglo-Saxon Bible until long after, no Anglo-Saxon books of devotion, as all theology was in the Greek or the Latin tongue, neither of which could be mastered at once; it is easy to see under what enormous disadvantages these Anglo-Saxon clergy would labour. What a contrast for the worse would they present to the monks! Uncouth, ignorant, unlearned, they would at first be entrusted with the inferior offices only of the ministry—perhaps to baptize, to visit the sick, to collect the alms of the faithful. They would be sent to outlying hamlets and distant villages, where the bishop or the monk never appeared; and thus, an inferior class from the very first, their ministrations would be confined to an inferior class of the laity.

So the result is such as might have been anticipated. Kings and nobles enter the cloisters; kings' sons become monks and abbots, kings' daughters nuns and lady abbesses. No noble, no prince becomes a parochial clergyman. The monasteries engross universal favour. For them gifts and offerings are made in rich abundance. Nobles and kings vie with each other in munificence to the "religious." Theirs are the broad acres, the mills, the fish-ponds; theirs also the embroidery, the jewellery, the gold and silver plate, the relics of all the civilization saved from the shipwreck of ancient society. Theirs are the surest and the safest of all depositories for the living and the dead, for the riches of this world and of the world to come.

There was one other advantage the monks enjoyed—it may seem to us a little one, too little to be noticed by grave historians—but such trifles determine the ocean currents of history. Monasteries had exclusively the right of sepulture within their walls. There only was an inviolable asylum for the dead, a final resting-place that could not be disturbed, amidst this holy brotherhood, with whose prayers the memories of the dead ascended to Heaven, and in whose holiness their sins were blotted out and forgiven. As yet there were no parochial churchyards under the shadow of the parochial church. And if there had been, who could be sure that they would be respected? Who could tell, in the perpetual disturbances of the times, how soon they might pass into pagan hands or be converted to profane uses? In distant hamlets what should repress the hand of the spoiler? So monasteries had a double grasp upon the population. Nowhere else in this life did such solemn accents of prayer and praise ascend to Heaven, nowhere else did the dead, sanctified by their hallowed resting-place, seem so surely to have passed.

"Through shades and silent rest to endless joy."

This exclusive privilege brought numerous advantages. Kings, nobles, and prelates purchased the right of interment among the monks, by gifts of land and various acts of munificence; people of lower rank, by mortuary fees of the most costly kind. The horse and his trappings which came with the corpse, the car and apparel of the yeoman, the mantle and arms of the soldier fell to the possession of the monasteries.

HOW THE CHRISTIAN RELIGION WAS TAUGHT. 47

They increased rapidly in wealth and number. They monopolized the alms, the offerings, the favour of all ranks. The clergy were wholly eclipsed by them, the authority of the bishops overshadowed. So at the commencement of the eighth century the historian complains that in consequence of such unwise liberality, not a spot was left where a new See could be erected, although the growing wants of the Church greatly demanded an increase of the episcopate. The rage for a monastic life had become so common, its secular advantages so tempting, that he anticipated the time when, from the decay of true religion, consequent upon the paucity of its ministers, and the decreasing military forces of the nation, there would be no effectual defence against a barbarian invasion.[1]

His anticipations were soon to be realized. In A.D. 787, the Danes landed for the first time at Weymouth, near Dorchester,[2] and from that date until nearly the close of the next century, they ceased not to ravage England with fire and sword. As plunder was their main object their

[1] Bede, Epistle to Egbert, Bishop of York, § 11. He became bishop A.D. 732. Bede, who was himself a monk, died A.D. 735.

[2] They landed here from three ships, as the Anglo-Saxons had done before them; and the one is no more an instance of a mystical number than the other. Flor. Wigorn. sub an.

fury was chiefly directed against the monasteries, where the wealth and treasure of the nation had been gathered up. The monasteries were burnt and destroyed, their inmates dispersed. The fascination they had exercised upon the religious feelings of the nation was dispelled. Necessity imposed other exertions. Alfred and his successors had to build ships and forts to provide for the material security of the nation; and monasteries, for a time, were forgotten.

CHAPTER IV.

COMMENCEMENT OF PAROCHIAL CHURCHES.

WHEN therefore the monasteries were destroyed and the monks killed or dispersed, the burthen of maintaining the faith and keeping Christianity alive, in the troubles and distresses of the times, fell wholly on the bishops and the secular, or, as we should now call them, the parochial clergy. As cities and monasteries offered the surest hopes of plunder, they were the chief objects of attack.[1] The bishops were driven from their cathedrals, the clergy from the populous towns; and once more we witness the same

[1] "The monuments still remain," says the author of the Abingdon Chronicle, "of the subversion of cities, the burning of villages, the destruction of monasteries; and their ruins may yet be seen at this day. When peace was restored, the places occupied by previous cultivators, who fled during the troubles, fell into the hands of other masters, and the proprietorship and tenantry were changed." Abingdon Chron. i. 37.

phenomenon as we have noticed already. Christianity is shaken out from the cities in which it had been gathered up, and dispersed in the rural and less accessible districts. The old diocesan arrangement of the bishop and his college of priests residing together, is in a great measure broken up by the necessities of the age. Their intercourse is interrupted. Each one is now compelled to shift for himself. So by degrees priests begin to settle here and there, and take up their permanent abode in different parts of the diocese. And as there is no longer a common fund for their support—for wherever the diocesan tithes can still be collected, they are paid to the bishop and the cathedral church— these priests become dependent for their maintenance chiefly on the alms and oblations of their congregations.

Hitherto of little or no account, and totally eclipsed by the monastic orders, they now begin to stand higher in public estimation. Taken mainly from the lower ranks of the people, for no one who could be admitted into a monastery would become a rural priest, they had been held in little respect, and probably had little education.[2] Even their diocesans, generally selected

[2] The Council at Clyffe (A.D. 747) enjoins upon all priests to learn and explain in the vulgar tongue the Lord's Prayer

COMMENCEMENT OF PAROCHIAL CHURCHES. 51

from the monks for their learning, would have preferred to the higher offices of the Church one of their own order, if he could be had, to the neglect of the secular priest; in other words, one who had been well trained and educated in the monastery, to one who had been ordained from the laity, with little or no learning. So strongly were people impressed by this sentiment, that whereas by the laws of the Anglo-Saxons, a regular priest, that is, a priest who was also a monk, was considered equal in rank to a thane or one of the minor nobility, a secular priest was reckoned no higher than a deacon of the same order.[2] But now this was impossible. The monks were dispersed. Such as survived the massacre of the Danes returned to the world; and whilst the care of maintaining religion fell exclusively into the hands of the secular clergy, the bishops were constrained to look to them only for the work of the ministry. Thus the secular or parochial clergy gained respect and influence they never possessed before. By degrees they were not only established in various parts of the rural districts, but advanced to places of dignity in the metropolitan churches,

and the Apostles' Creed, and to master the meaning of the words used in the two Sacraments. Can. 10.

[2] Laws of Ethelred. Anglo-Saxon Laws, i. 345.

E 2

until they were dispossessed of their honours and emoluments under Dunstan and Edgar.

But in the interval an event took place which cannot be passed over in silence. Every one knows that of all the endowments of the Church of England tithes are regarded as the most considerable. If they did not constitute the sole maintenance of the bishops and their clergy, as distinct from the monasteries, in the days of St. Augustine and his successors, it is quite certain that they formed no unimportant part of it. Yet tithes are seldom noticed in the scanty records of these earlier ages. Bishops at the first being uniformly monks, and incapable of holding property, had little or no need of their own share of the tithes.[4] If they were strict in enforcing them, it was for the poor, the clergy, the repair of their churches.[5] But churches and cathedrals in those early ages were of the poorest

---

[4] Thus of Aidan, the Bishop of Lindisfarne, Bede remarks: "Aidan, the first bishop of that place, was a monk, and throughout his life strictly observed the monastic rule. From his time to the present all the bishops so exercise their episcopal office, that whilst the abbot, elected with consent of the brotherhood, rules the monastery, the priests, deacons, and all the rest of every ecclesiastical degree, the bishop included, pay obedience to the monastic rule. And this," he says, "was the command given by Pope Gregory to St. Augustine." Vit. S. Cuthberti, ch. xvi.

[5] [See note, p. 156.]

description, and in the greater magnificence of the monastic churches attracted little care and little attention. It was not until they obtained the right of sepulture, when piety and affection to the dead buried within their walls stimulated the survivors to raise memorials in their honour, that churches and cathedrals assumed a greater splendour. In later times the estates and the manors attached to the Sees, sometimes by regal or noble personages, more frequently by the archbishops and bishops themselves, provided a much larger income than any derived from tithes.[6] The clergy, on the other hand, properly so called, for whom Gregory required that provision should be made outside monasteries, at first supported by the tithes and offerings, and dependent on the bishop, were now scattered by the fury of the Danes, and in a great measure cut off from this provision, if not independent of it.

In the year 855, in the very thick of their invasion, Ethelwulf, king of Wessex, that is, of all the provinces south of the Thames, with the exception of Kent and Cornwall, the son of

---

[6] Of this there can be no stronger proof than that the Archbishop of Canterbury in the year 822, consented to accept one hundred mansuri (small tenements with land attached) in the place of three hundred of which he had been deprived. Spelman's Concil. i. 333.

Egbert and the father of Alfred gave a tithe of his land, or rather the tenth acre of his lands, throughout his kingdom, free of all royal service and tribute, to the Church. It has been much disputed whether this grant was intended to apply to the whole of England, over which this king exercised a nominal supremacy, or exclusively to the kingdom of Wessex, or only, which is more probable, to his demesne and hereditary estates.[7] Except as an indication of the pious intentions of the king and his devotion to the Church, the whole question, though hotly

[7] See the Charters in Kemble's "A. S. Diplom." ii. nn. 270. 275, 276. Of those charters the third is admitted to be genuine by the editor, the other two are marked as spurious; though why, it is not easy to understand. Had the grant been made to a single monastery, or even to the monastic bodies at all, which at that time hardly existed, and certainly at that time never received tithes nor were supported by them, the doubt might have been reasonable. But Mr. Kemble, never being able to emancipate himself from the vulgar error of mistaking monks for ecclesiastics, has continually confounded the Church with the religious orders; not the only fatal blunder he has committed. Independently of the charter the fact is notorious, and is confirmed not only by all the chroniclers, but by Asser, the contemporary of King Alfred, who could scarcely have been mistaken.

Discrepancies in the dates and phraseology of these charters must not be pressed too far. They are not taken professedly from the originals, but generally from the pages of some individual chronicler, who probably did not consider himself bound,

contested by lawyers and antiquarians, is of no importance whatever. The tithes and endowments, now held by the Church of England, are not derived from this, or any other royal grant or confirmation, but came from a totally different source, as will be shown in the sequel. As a legal document, if such it can be called, it was altogether invalid. A general grant to the Church, where no Church was specified, and no penalty attached to its infringement, was of no worth whatever. A grant of tithe in the land, when the Danes were driving all before them, was, in its material advantages to the Church, of little value. Who was to collect the produce, when it was raised, or enforce the payment? As for the establishment of a right, tithes had been collected in Wessex long before.[8] We can then only regard it as a pious intention on the part of the king; perhaps as an atonement for his neglect in contributing what he felt was only due to God's service—the sense of which was forced upon him by the troubles and distractions into which his kingdom had fallen.

provided he retained the substance, like other historians, to adhere rigidly to every word and phrase of the original.

[8] See the Pan-Anglican Council of Chelcheth, in which the Kings of Kent, Mercia, Wessex, and Northumberland took part, and confirmed its decrees, A.D. 787. Can. 17.

The royal city of Wessex, and its surrounding district, were still under the control of a single bishop. The tithes granted by Ethelwulf would be exclusively paid, if they were levied at all, into the bishop's fund for the spiritual wants of the diocese—to maintain, if possible, the dying embers of Christianity, nearly extinguished by the Danes.

From that date however the payment of tithes is continually insisted on :—by King Alfred, and Alfred and Godrun,[9] by Edward the Elder,[1] by Athelstan,[2] by Edward,[3] by Edgar,[4] by Ethelred,[5] by Canute,[6] by Edward the Confessor.[7] As we advance to the era of the Norman Conquest these injunctions become more explicit. Priests are commanded to preach them to the people. Penalties are attached to their infringement, and directions are given for punishing the offenders. As a further inducement to collect them, the bishops in the middle of the eleventh century gave up their claim to tithes altogether, and allowed them to be settled entirely on the district or

---

[9] Præf. ad Leges, § 38.   Leges Eccles. cap. 9.
[1] Leges Eccl. c. 6.
[2] Council at Greatanlea, sub. init. and Leg. Eccl. c. 1.
[3] Leg. Eccl. c. 2.   [4] Leg. Eccl. c. 1.
[5] Leg. Eccl. c. 4.
[6] Epist. ad Proceres, and Leg. Eccl. c. 8.
[7] Leg. Eccl. c. 8.

parochial churches.[8] Such repeated injunctions do not show any great alacrity in the payment of tithes, however the Anglo-Saxon kings and their Wittenagemotes might desire it. Nor, strange to say, was the neglect chargeable on the laity alone. "Tithes," say the Laws of the Confessor, "are to be paid to God; and whoever detains them shall be compelled to make them good, by the justice of the bishop and king, if need be. These (tithes) St. Augustine preached and taught, and these were conceded by the king, the lords, and the people. But afterwards, by the instigation of the devil, many detained them; and rich priests, growing negligent, would not trouble themselves with looking after them, because they had enough for the necessities of life. Moreover in many places there are now three or four churches, when at that time there was one only, and so they have diminished."[9]

We have here the whole reason of the thing plainly set before us. Tithes were not paid in

[8] "The Holy Fathers have determined that men shall pay their tithes to the Church of God, and give them to the priest, who is to divide them into three parts; one for the repair of the church, another for the poor, and a third for the minister." Thus the bishops resigned their ancient right to the fourth part. Canons of Ælfric, § 24. [See note, p. 156.]

[9] Leg. Eccl. c. 9.

money but in kind :—the tithe sheaf, the tithe calf, the tithe pig. So long as the bishop lived with his college of priests around him, tithe in kind supplied their tables, or could be sold in the great cities, where the bishop and his clergy resided. So long as the monasteries stood, prior to the invasion of the Danes, they too no doubt would serve as markets. But what could the priest, in distant rural districts, do with his tithe produce, when the roads were infested with Danes and marauders? What chance would he have of compelling a powerful thane, or a Danish Earl, like Godwin or Harold, or their favourites, to pay him their tithe?[1] Moreover, as I have already explained, the tithes and offerings did not belong to the priest but to the bishop, or rather to the common fund of the diocese, and therefore the priest had no predominant interest in collecting them—rather the reverse. And as by degrees the ancient system was broken up, and the clergy were beginning to settle permanently in the country,

---

[1] Even as late as William the Conqueror the road from St. Alban's to London was so much infested by bears, wolves, and robbers, that the monks could not send their produce to London in safety, or bring from the city what they wanted. Gesta Abb. S. Albani, i. 39, ed. Riley. What then must have been the state of other parts of England?

the diocesan fund was less required. Bishops as we have seen,[1] gave up their part of it, and the parish priests, otherwise provided for, ceased to look to it for their maintenance. What that provision was I shall explain hereafter.

One chief means of support was the right of sepulture, consequent upon the destruction of the monasteries. So long as they stood, no privilege was so earnestly coveted as that of burial within the monastic precincts. It was desired all the more, not merely because of the high estimation for sanctity in which such places were held by the Anglo-Saxons, but because of their fancied immunity from profanation. Whilst other spots might become the battle-ground of rival factions, and pass from one Kingdom of the Heptarchy into the dominion of another, be converted to secular uses, at best subject to spoliation—a monastic house, it was supposed, would always be respected, whether the conqueror were a king of Wessex, or an Anglian, or a Mercian. No one anticipated a time when a pagan spoiler, like the Dane, should specially turn his rage and avarice against the religious houses, and rifle shrines and tombs for their ornaments, scattering to the winds the relics of saints, and the bones of kings

[1] [p. 56, *ante.*]

and prelates, that had rested there for centuries.[2] Besides the rites for the dead could be performed by the whole convent with much greater solemnity than by a poor priest in his single person.[3] The privilege was a source of no small profit to the religious houses, not merely for the mortuary fees, which were considerable, but because the wealthy and the noble frequently left valuable bequests of land or other property to the houses where they wished to be buried. Sometimes also, if the bishops or priests were unmarried, as most were, they bequeathed the whole of their property to the monastery or church or college selected for their interment.

But when the monasteries were sacked and desecrated by the Danes, who left nothing behind them but the bare walls and smoking ruins, their privilege of sepulture was extinguished, and was

[2] In St. Augustine's Abbey at Canterbury, St. Augustine, his successors, and all the kings of Kent were buried in succession until the year 758, when Archbishop Cuthbert contrived to break through the rule, and have himself buried by his own monks, in his own cathedral. Still the privilege was not immediately extinguished. Thomas of Elmham, Hist. Monast. S. Augustini, p. 317, ed. Hardwicke.

[3] Probably there was another reason derived from remote antiquity. As the Anglo-Saxons were buried with chain-armour and ornaments, their graves were dug very deep, as they are now, compared with graves on the Continent, to prevent them from being rifled.

COMMENCEMENT OF PAROCHIAL CHURCHES. 61

not generally revived until after the Norman Conquest. Yet the desire of being buried in consecrated ground was as strong as ever; and the fees for burial now fell to the priesthood.

Moreover, within a very short period of the Norman Conquest, the Church had grown so strict in prohibiting burials within the walls, that is to say, in the city churches, that the rural cemeteries became the only places of interment, and the advantages attached to them were more valuable to the officiating minister than ever, far more than any tithe could have been. "It was an old custom," say the authors of the Ecclesiastical Institutes of the Anglo-Saxons,[4] "in these lands, often to bury departed men within the church, and convert into cemeteries the places which were hallowed to God's service, and blessed for offering to Him. Now we will not allow, henceforth, any one to be buried within the church, unless he be of the priesthood, or is so righteous a layman, that it is well known, that in his life he merited by his conduct such a place for his corpse to rest in. We will not, however, that the bodies so buried be cast out, but the graves shall either be dug deeper, or covered over, and the pavement shall be evenly laid. But if in any place (church)

[4] P. 409, ed. Thorpe.

there be so many graves that this cannot easily be done, let it be left as a cemetery, and the altar be taken thence and set in a chosen place, and a (new) church be raised there for God's service."

Thus from many places, where there had once been district or parochial churches, the altar was removed, and they became nothing more than cemeteries or mortuary chapels; and chapels, as will presently appear, being consecrated by bishops and possessing consecrated altars, were erected in parochial churches for God's service.[5] So chapels, with their cemeteries annexed, became valuable acquisitions. "If a thane," say the Laws of King Edgar,[6] "have a church on his land with a cemetery, he shall give a third part of his own tithes to his church."[7] That is to say, he shall be at liberty to give one-third of his tithes to the church standing on his own property, paying the other two-thirds to the mother church of his parish. But, continues the law,

---

[5] See Abingdon Chron. i. 475.—People seem possessed with a notion that churches were built first and churchyards added to them for the benefit of the parish. History and law point to the opposite conclusion. The cemetery existed long before there was any parish or any parish church, and therefore the parish could have originally no right to it.

[6] Anglo-Saxon Laws, i. 263, ed. Thorpe. Repeated by Canute.

[7] Because one-third of the tithe was the priest's portion. See the Laws of Ethelred, Ang.-Sax. L. i. 343.

"if he have a church, to which there is no cemetery attached, then shall he give his priest what he will of the nine parts, and pay all his dues to the old minster," or mother church. In other words, he shall pay his tithes to the parish church, giving his own chaplain or minister what he likes of the remaining nine parts of his property.

So, then, instead of having one general and uniform ecclesiastical system established, still less one grand national endowment of churches to the service of God, by some national act, we have, as might be expected, a Church of varied organization, the parts of which, like all living organizations, are in a different stage of development. It has attained to its present station and greatness, not full-feathered and fledged from any royal, national, or parliamentary nursery; but like the material fabric in which it was enshrined, some portions were changed, others augmented and developed as occasion allowed or necessity demanded. "All churches," say the Laws of Canute, "are not entitled to the same worldly estimation." [8] And he proceeds to distinguish them, according to their fine or compensation, into the chief minster, which stood at the head, the subordinate (parish church) which was one half

---

[8] See Ang.-Sax. Laws, i. 361. Repeated with some variation by Henry I.

below the former in estimation, the small parish church with a cemetery annexed where service was less frequently performed, and the rural chapel which was lowest in the scale.

Thus, here and there, by slow degrees, parish churches and chapels sprang up in various parts of England. In some the minister was still supported out of the diocesan fund, and still paid the tithes and offerings to the bishop of the diocese, if required. In others, again, the incumbent, by leave of the bishop, distributed the tithes, paying one part to himself, and two parts to the necessities of his church and the parish.[1] Others, again, were supported by the mortuary fees arising from the cemetery annexed. Others, by glebe-land varying in amounts from 25 to 200 acres. Others, simply by the fees arising from the religious services and customary offerings. Again, some of these churches were erected by the bishop, or by one or other of his clergy with the bishop's consent; others by the thane or his freemen, on his estate. Nowhere did uniformity prevail throughout. Nowhere was any general system established, and least of all by the nation. Whilst in some places, like Worcester, there was only one " Minster church " and a vicarage, in another, like Norwich, there were forty-three chapels in the hands of the burgesses.

[1] [See note, p. 156.]

Whilst in some counties, like Lincolnshire, there were as many as 131 parish priests, and in Yorkshire 136, there were none in Bedfordshire, Buckinghamshire, or Surrey. Whilst there were 222 churches in Lincolnshire, 243 in Norfolk, and 364 in Suffolk, there were none in Middlesex. Whilst tithes were paid to the priest or parochial church in other parts of England, none are recorded in Somersetshire, Devonshire, Cornwall, Middlesex, Hertfordshire or Leicestershire.[9] In one county the churches were of wood and thatch, in another of stone. Here were priests without

[9] These statements are derived from the Domesday Survey, made by William the Conqueror, A.D. 1083. According to the estimate then taken, it is computed that there were about 1700 churches and chapels and 995 priests. It is worth observing that the churches were most numerous in the Anglian, and after the Danish settlements, in the East Coast, another indication of their wealth. Lincolnshire, Suffolk, and Norfolk were rated highly for Peter-pence. It would seem, then, as if the Danes spared their own countrymen and wasted the western and inland counties. Allowing that there may have been mistakes and omissions in Domesday, yet so far as the statements in the text are concerned, it may be accepted as sufficiently correct. [Mr. Brewer was of course aware, that no return of churches was required in the Precept in obedience to which Domesday was compiled. See Sir Hy. Ellis's Introuction to Domesday, p. xci. He had no doubt satisfied himself of the accuracy of Domesday, so far as the statements in the text are concerned, by collateral authorities the nature of which could not be stated in a brief note. L.T.D.]

churches, and there churches without resident priests. Here two or three priests were attached to one church, and there more than one church was served by one priest.

CHAPTER V.

THE ORIGIN AND HISTORY OF THE PRESENT TITHES AND ENDOWMENTS OF THE CHURCH OF ENGLAND.

The period we have passed through was one of perpetual battle and confusion, the nation vainly endeavouring to emerge from disorder into consistency and unity, and never completely succeeding in the effort. The unceasing contentions and wars of the age may deserve some better title than Milton's contemptuous description of them, as "the battles of kites and crows," and we may hope that the gross vices and degeneracy into which all classes of the nation were said to have fallen were somewhat exaggerated by contemporary historians.[1] Still the undoubted

[1] It might be thought that the Chroniclers of the times were too partial to the Normans and unjust to the Anglo-Saxons, but the evidence furnished by their own laws cannot be suspected. From them we learn that the churches were ill-served

fact remains, that whilst the Anglo-Saxons on their arrival could only gain possession of the island, after repeated efforts and many years of warfare, they lost it in a single battle. The whole land passed at once into the hands of the Norman, and not a struggle, worthy of the name, was made by them to recover their independence. With strong local and individual attachments there was no sense of national unity among them; no power, and apparently no wish, to build up a strong, compact, and mighty people. So from the first hour when they settled themselves in Kent until the nominal consolidation of the Heptarchy under Egbert, they ceased not

and stripped of all decencies (Ang. Sax. Laws, ii. 341); that they were employed for storing corn and hay (ib. 407). Moreover the assertion of Malmesbury that the English nobles did not go to church, but had the service gabbled over by chaplains in their bedchambers, has more the air of veracity than is generally supposed. For he refers to a practice, the Church found some difficulty in suppressing, of every man of rank appointing a private chaplain, until, from vanity and imitation, every one did the same, so encouraging a class of ill-taught and shifty clergymen, and withdrawing the dues from the parish church. But the foulest blot was their habit of selling their slaves, both male and female, and that under circumstances intolerably disgraceful. So in a Synod held at London (A.D. 1102) we find the following canon:—
"Let no one exercise that nefarious traffick whereby heretofore men in *England* were sold like brute cattle."

to fight among themselves, " who should be the greatest," with as deadly and relentless animosity as they had fought against the Britons. From the supposed supremacy of Egbert, until within six years of Alfred's death, the whole country was kept in a state of perpetual trembling by the Danes, who carried fire and sword into every great town of the kingdom. And though these Danes were but a handful as compared with the Anglo-Saxons, and scourged every coast, and carried their ravages into every part of England, yet the nation never could be roused into one great effort to dislodge and repel them. A short interval of peace, purchased in fact by the cession of all the Eastern provinces to the Danes, who from enemies thus became the advanced guard of England, was followed by a renewed attack of the same people, which ended in placing a Pagan and a Dane on the Christian throne of Alfred, and finally paved the way for the vigorous rule and policy of the Norman.

The bare sketch of such a state of things will show how impossible it was for any consistent or uniform system of government to develope itself, whether legislative or executive. Not only in earlier times, but practically to the time of the Conquest, the provinces north of the

Humber were independent of those south of the Humber to the Thames (the Mercians); whilst the people south of the Thames were independent of both, and all three of the East Anglian provinces, that is, of the east of England, as well as of Cornwall, Wales, and Cumberland in the west. The Mercian had his own laws and customs, and would not submit to those of the Northumbrian; the Northumbrian rejected those of Wessex. The Dane had his own laws, ranks, and institutions, and despised the Anglo-Saxon. Irregularity prevailed everywhere. Disorder in the frame-work of society was reflected in the morals of society;—brigandage was common, and could only be suppressed by the severest measures of the Conqueror. Idleness, luxury, drunkenness, and licentiousness—vices which had led to the destruction of the Britons—were now equally active in making the Anglo-Saxon a comparatively easy conquest for the Norman.

It was not to be expected that the Church should be exempted from the ill effects of the same influences. *Ut populus sic sacerdos.* The old diocesan system, already described, had broken down, and no other had yet risen to take its place. The discipline of the clergy had been greatly relaxed, when foreign war or internal dissensions severed the relation between them and the bishop. The destruction of the monasteries, in one sense advantageous, was in another disastrous, as the channels of learning and education were thus dried up. No books existed elsewhere, no manuscripts could be perpetuated without their aid. "So completely," says King Alfred, "had learning perished from the land, that there were very few on this side of the Humber who could explain their Common Prayers in the English tongue, or translate any Latin passage into English;—so few indeed, that I cannot remember any one south of the Thames, at the time when I came to the throne."[2]

Matters had not much improved in the century before the Conquest. Many of the clergy, taken from the lower ranks of the smaller yeomanry, were in education, manners, and culture little superior. During the destruction of the monasteries, the bishops had to supply the places of the monks by secular clergy. From these preferments they were dislodged by the Archbishops Odo and Dunstan, backed by the

---

[2] Preface to Gregory's Pastorale. The complaint is repeated by Elfric shortly before the Conquest. He states in the preface to his grammar that, until the revival of monasticism by Dunstan, the priesthood were so ignorant that they could neither translate nor write a Latin letter.

power of Edgar, with ignominy and disgrace—an ungrateful return for their former services. It was pretended that they were non-resident; that they neglected the services of the cathedral; that they were in point of strictness and religious duties far inferior to the monastic orders; that as married men their wives and children occupied their thoughts, and set an example of worldly distraction, incompatible with the solemnity and sanctity of the cloister. Their removal was a blow to the parochial clergy, as it excluded them from all hopes of honourable preferment and lowered them once again in the estimation of the people. As all avenues to reward and distinction were in the main closed against them, none who expected either entered their ranks; whilst the ardent and devout naturally turned to the monastery as more in accordance with their aspirations.

This then is the state of things at the era of the Conquest; a rural clergy, of mean attainments and rank in the main, the companions and teachers of the villein, the bondmen and bondwomen, the serf, the cottier, the lowest cultivators of the soil; holding among them a small portion of land, too small to be specified in the Great Survey of the Kingdom.[3] How such an

[3] Thus after enumerating the larger tenants and free men,

endowment had come to the priest cannot be absolutely determined in all cases. Sometimes he had bought it; sometimes it had been given by the lord of the fee or district; sometimes by a few of his tenantry. It had been the free gift of one man or more, like any other charitable gift; like the lands or estates of a hospital. The tithes he may or may not have had, as the case might be; for even if legally due to him, he had no power to enforce them. If he could prevail on some great Danish Earl or powerful Norman Baron, who cared nothing for him or his Anglo-Saxon laws,[1] to pay his dues, he

---

we find the compilers of Doomsday entering such notices as these:—

"8 villeins, 10 cottagers, and a priest hold 5½ ploughlands" (i.e. a variable quantity, as much as could be ploughed in a day).

Again—"8 villeins, 5 cottagers, a priest, and a radchenister hold 9 plough-lands."

And again—"1 villein, a priest, and 3 bordarii (labourers) hold 2 plough-lands. 14 villeins and 1 priest hold 10 plough-lands," &c.

[1] [There are several Anglo-Saxon laws as to tithes still extant. Selden (ch. 8) enumerates the following: A.D. 786 Offa, king of Mercia, in a council of chief men, both ecclesiastical and lay; A.D. 900 Alfred the Great, confirmed by his son Edward and a council of wise men; A.D. 855 Ethelwulph, in a council of bishops and chief men; A.D. 930 Athelstan, with advice of bishops; A.D. 940 Edmund, in a

might consider himself more fortunate than most of his brethren. If then the tithes of the parochial clergy of the Church of England had been derived from these sources, and their payment had exclusively depended on the law, they might as well have never existed.

synod of lay and spiritual men; A.D. 970 Edgar, in a council of wise men and barons; A.D. 1010 Ethelred, by the advice of two archbishops; A.D. 1020 Canute the Dane; Edward the Confessor. There is great uncertainty as to the genuineness of some of these so-called laws, and still more as to their exact terms and meaning. While on the one hand they are appealed to as conclusive proof of the statutory origin of tithes, on the other they are considered as merely extending the protection of law to the possession of tithes already given to the Church. Thus Mr. Brewer writes in a MS. note: "A mere declaration of the law in favour of a certain right of property no more constitutes it a national gift than if that declaration had never been made, no more than the decision of a court of law in the case of individual property, nor shews more of a national origin in one case than in the other." See also pp. 127, 282 *note.* Perhaps the true place of the Anglo-Saxon laws in the history of tithes will be found to lie between these two extreme positions. It is in the highest degree improbable that no tithes were paid to the Church before these laws were made. But, on the other hand, it is difficult to believe that the framers of the laws did not intend to produce by their means an extension of the practice of tithe-paying, or that these laws did not in fact exert a powerful influence on the growth of the *custom,* and conduce to its development, in a later age, into a legal *right.*—L.T.D.]

The true history of modern tithes and endowments is this: "At first the bishop and his presbyters resided at the cathedral church, to which the Christians of the whole diocese did at solemn times resort, and had there alone the public offices of religion. Only some priests of the cathedral college were by the bishop's designation sent out as itinerant preachers through the remoter parts of the country, to convert and instruct, and after their appointed circuit to return to their common place of residence.[4] This missionary practice could have no excuse but the necessity of those times. For the inconveniences were great and many." Such was the imperfect instruction of the people— the little knowledge the priest could obtain by his casual visits of the state of his flock—the hurried and intermittent administration of Holy Baptism—and the visitation of the sick. "Yet under these difficulties," continues our author, "our nation might still have laboured, if the nobility and gentry had not, in pity to their families and tenantry, erected some churches

[4] Precisely as certain dissenters do now. And as when the dissenters or Methodists have raised up an interest in their teaching in some new district, they get their new converts to build a chapel, with some aid from the Central Missionary Fund, and make provision for the minister, so did the Church of England in those early times.

within their respective demesnes, and ascertained (appointed) such portion of house and land as, with the voluntary oblations of the people, might be a sufficient maintenance for one fixed priest, and by course of equity and rules of the imperial law, did entitle the said generous benefactor to the right of advowson in his own built and endowed church.

"It is indeed probable that before this public charity of laymen, some few rural churches were erected by the bishops out of the common stock or by the contribution of the people. . . But, however, these were not properly parochial churches, nor had they any fixed presbyter appropriated to the service of them. But they were mere chapels of ease to the cathedral, and were but now and then supplied by itinerant preachers or priests, who at uncertain times appointed by the bishop went thither to pray and preach and receive the oblations of the people, and carry them back to the bishop and his cathedral college. It is further probable that our first converted kings did build churches or oratories in their country-seats or palaces, but neither had these royal chapels the nature of parochial churches, but served for the occasional use of the kings in their royal progress, and had the offices of religion performed by a moving chaplain no longer than the court resided. So that whatever examples of piety were first given by kings and bishops, yet parish churches and resident priests were, in a manner, purely owing to the lay nobility and gentry, who either repaired[5] [or allowed their tenants and freeholders to repair] the old auxiliary churches, or recommended new structures to the bishop's consecration (built new churches) and provided accommodation for one or more fixed priests, to take [permanent] charge of the neighbouring people, and make it a proper cure of souls."[6]

Not only had the founder of the church,

[5] Thus Robert D'Oyley, a powerful Norman noble, repaired the ruinous parochial churches in and out of Oxford in the reign of William I. (Abing. Chron. ii. 14). So also, a little before, two wealthy men built a chapel and cemetery at Worth, and got it consecrated by the bishop, on condition of providing an endowment for the clergyman. (Ibid. 30.) A similar instance is found at Peasemore in the reign of Henry I. (Ibid. 31). These chapels had small endowments, not more than two or three acres, with other donatives; but larger churches had 50 or 100 acres; whilst the priest of Hugh de Grentmaisnil, probably by the liberality of his great patron, held 250 acres. Doomsday, i. 169.

[6] Bishop Kennett "On Lay Patronage," p. 9, ed. S. T. Wood, 1850—an excellent little book, and very interesting. It should be in the hands of all the clergy. See also his ' Law of Impropriations," p. 5, and Selden "On Tithes," vi. § 3, and ix. 4, where the same account is given, substantially, as that in the text. Consult, however, Chapter VIII, p. 134.

within his own manor or demesnes the right of the patronage, but for his greater encouragement in these works of charity the bishop resigned all claim to the tithes, and permitted the patron to devote them exclusively to the use of his church and parish, stipulating only that one-third should be secured to the minister for his proper maintenance, whilst the rest should be devoted to the same purposes as before. Thus the whole tithes of the manor were paid to the parish church—were the free donation of the lord of the manor—and no longer diocesan as before. They were private endowments given by the owners of these estates for their own benefit and that of their family and tenantry for ever.[7] Consequently, as at this day, no one could have any claim on the services of the parish church or its minister, except the inhabitants of the

[7] "Every man, questionless, would have been the unwillinger to have specially endowed the Church founded for the holy use chiefly of him, his family and tenants, if withal he might not have had the liberty to have given his incumbent, there resident, a special and several maintenance, which could not have been, had the former community (i. e. diocesan) of the clergy's revenue still remained. Out of these lay foundations chiefly, doubtless, came those kind of parishes which at this day are in every diocese, their differences in quantity being originally out of the difference of the several circuits of the demesnes or territories possessed by the founders." Selden, p. 260.

manor. To confiscate their endowments, would not be, as people ignorantly suppose, merely to deprive the church of its maintenance, but to deprive the lords of the manors, or, as we should now call them, the squires of the parish, of the churches built by their forefathers, and of those ministerial services they had provided out of their own funds. It would not merely deprive the clergyman of his living, but the parish of the benefits secured for it by its former benefactors.[8] Of course, if a dissenter refuses to avail himself of the advantages thus offered him, that is his own affair; but he is guilty of the greatest tyranny and oppression, if, not satisfied with this liberty, he insists that I and others should also be deprived of the benefits intended and secured for us, because he dislikes them. That is the same as if a man who objected to hospitals should insist on pulling them down and taking away their endowments because he had an objection, in his own case, to their method of cure.

But to return to my narrative. This mode of

[8] So far from the nation having built or endowed churches in its corporate capacity, the people of England generally contributed neither to one nor the other. They enjoy the use of churches built for them either by the bishops or the lay patrons, to which they have not been called upon to make any contribution in the way of tithes or endowments.

securing their tithes to the minister, proceeding from the lords of the manors themselves, had the effect of improving the condition of the parochial clergy by leaving them dependent no longer on voluntary and precarious support. The lord of the manor and his successors, both for their own sakes and those of their tenantry and dependants, took care to see that the minister should not be defrauded. Their personal presence and influence had more authority than any laws, which could never have commanded respect, if the lay body had not been interested in seeing them respected.

The Anglo-Saxons were careless and slovenly; their whole system of government, judicature, and defence,—uncertain, slow, and unwieldly. Never prepared to meet their enemies, they were easily conquered—and easily disconcerted, notwithstanding their personal bravery, when opposed to a nimble and active adversary. On the other hand the Normans, systematic and precise, decisive in their movements, costly in their dress, nice in their food, sumptuous in their buildings, carried the same love of order, and the same discipline into all the relations of life. The face of the nation was as rapidly changed, as a country lout, under the hands of a recruiting serjeant, with some trouble and grumbling, is transformed into a smart, clean-shaven and orderly soldier.[9] The whole country became like a great garrison. The Church itself could not escape from the same influence, and was not allowed if it would. The bishops, now generally Normans, exempted from attendance in the county courts, could devote themselves more exclusively to superintending their clergy—and carried into the Church the rigid discipline of their countrymen. The Conquest was, in this respect, as beneficial to the clergy as it was to the laity. So new churches and monasteries sprang up in all directions; the older and more humble fabrics were rebuilt with greater magnificence; and the old notion—so pleasantly alluded to in Addison's description of Sir Roger de Coverley, where the old knight and patron of the living looks round to see that the clergymen and his tenants are doing their duty—then first took its beginning.[1]

What better method could be devised for

---

[9] The whole art of war was derived from the Normans, and with it habits of discipline were carried into all ranks of society.

[1] "Spectator," No. 112. According to the old notion, the parish is the miniature of the diocese; and as the king's supremacy is acknowledged by the bishop, that of the lay patron was respected by the rector, and he alone was permitted a seat within the chancel.

binding all classes together in one common union of great and permanent interest? How could religious instruction and consolation be more efficiently secured for the poor labourer, the bondman, and the serf, than by thus bringing the Gospel to their doors, and providing for them gratuitously a resident teacher? Unable to help themselves, separated by a wide and impassable interval from their great lords, who understood neither their language nor their wants, and were constantly absent in war, there could be no greater benefactor, no better guide than their parish priest. Superior to his hearers by position and education, placed by a moderate endowment beyond the necessity of worldly occupations, supplied with the means of dispensing charity, the centre of his flock, the interpreter and mediator between the rich and poor, between the conquered and their masters, what better institution could human forethought, sagacity, or statesmanship have devised for the miseries and necessities of the age? What method could the heart or imagination of man have conceived better calculated to bind together in one harmonious bond the antagonistic extremes of society —the head of gold and the toes of clay?

Here, then, without the expenditure of a shilling from the national treasury, without any effort on the part of the State, a body of men was established in every parish and remote corner of England, devoted to the spiritual welfare and service of their fellow-men. In whatever condition those men might be—lords of extensive domains, or bound to the soil in hopeless slavery —they found in the parish priest one common adviser and teacher, alike acceptable to both in the common necessities of humanity. Confined to his flock, yet independent by this salutary provision of their prejudices and caprice, he was not compelled to forfeit that dignity and independence which are indispensable to those who must at times correct and reprimand as well as advise. Shut out by the sanctity of his calling from the paths of ambition and the pursuit of wealth, he could devote himself, without distraction, to his duties, exempt from the servile and degrading necessity of flattering his congregation through dread of their displeasure, or experiencing their resentment if he spoke with authority. So in a state of society, rough, rude and oppressive, in proportion as it descended to the lower strata on which it rested, where laws never assumed a benevolent aspect, and charity had not yet extended its soothing influences, the parish priest could teach mankind to realize in the Church, of which all alike were members, that universal fellowship and brotherhood of which they experienced so little in the world around them.[2] He could by precept and example enforce the lesson of resignation and contentment—a much purer heroism and saintship than all the vaunted examples of philosophy—in a state of society where the great mass of mankind could never possess more than the bitter and unequal portion of badly remunerated toil and privation, without any of the worldly fruits.

In the social and moral influences of the parochial clergy—to say nothing of their religious influences—who can fail to see the incalculable advantages reaped by this arrangement? How much is due to them for that general stability, patience, and forbearance, not yet entirely lost to us, without which life would be intolerable, and every reform would degenerate into revolution!

It must not, however, be imagined that the system here described started forth all at once in full vigour and perfection; or that the

---

[2] This is perfectly clear in the guilds and fraternities of the middle ages, all of which had a religious basis, many of them a common altar and a common priest. Fraternity, equality, trades-unionism, except on that basis, are a delusion and mischievous juggle.

Church and nation immediately emerged from its former confusion, when William took possession of the Crown. He was imperious and arbitrary, deposing bishop and abbots at his pleasure, and depriving both of their manors and their property. Even his queen, Matilda, did not scruple to extort from the religious houses their jewels and ornaments.[3] His officers followed their lord's example, and showed little regard to the discomfited English, whom they despised, whether lay or clerical. Norman bishops could not sympathize with the poor parochial clergy, whose language they did not understand, and whose attainments they treated with contempt. Even then, had they been so inclined, the clergy in the rural districts, deprived of their natural protectors, could do little to resist the arbitrary acts of their conquerors, or secure their own rights against such powerful oppressors. In some instances they were dispossessed, and their benefices, if

---

[3] As in the case of the Abbey of Abingdon; and when the abbot and his monks laid before her Majesty some of their choicer ornaments, she insisted on more costly ones; and in the end was satisfied with nothing less than a chasuble embroidered with gold work, a choral cope, a white stole, and a copy of the Gospels bound with gold and precious stones. Chron. Abingd. i. 485.

valuable, given to Norman chaplains. In others, the tithes were diverted to alien purposes, or sold, or farmed, or pensions were reserved out of them for the patrons.[4] As in the disorders of the times there were many poor and ignorant priests, it was easy for the patron to hire a vicar by the year, and by the payment of a small pension take all the profits of the living to himself, or share them with the vicar. For whether the Norman noble built the church, or provided its endowments, or it had come into his possession by distribution of the conquered lands, it was no more than natural that he should regard the church and its endowments in the same light as the rest of his property, and dispose of them at his pleasure, especially when the churches stood in his own domain.[5]

[4] Thus it is stated in the Chronicle of Battle that in the time of the Conqueror any one might dispose of his tithes where he pleased, p. 27; and elsewhere that the lay lords who obtained grants of vills and manors under the Norman kings, with churches attached to them, claimed the right of advowson; "for," said they, "the Church is the head of the vill and more worthy than all the body." Ib. 128.

[5] Thus before the close of the eleventh century we find various complaints of the sale of churches by laymen, clerks, and monks (Order. Vit. p. 528), and consequently a variety

These evils were by care and time removed, but they were succeeded by others more disastrous to the parochial clergy. Even before their arrival in England the Normans had been great benefactors to religious houses in their own country. They followed the same custom here. Their two great archbishops, Lanfranc and Anselm, were monks; and the first act of William was to build a monastery at Battle, in Sussex, in commemoration of his victory.

of injunctions, that no layman shall have any part of the altar offerings, or fees for burial, or the third part of the tithes, or take money for the sale of them, or remove a priest from his living without consent of the bishop. (Ibid. 552.)

In 1102 it is ordered that tithes shall be given to none but to churches, that churches shall not be sold, that no chapel shall be built without leave of the bishop, or church consecrated without due provision for the minister, and that no monks shall accept of churches without the bishop's consent, or deprive them of their revenues. Spelman, Con. ii. 22.

In 1173 children are not to be admitted to cure of souls, nor laymen to take any portion of the Church's offerings, "or appoint annual vicars," or deduct any part of the parson's tithe. In 1195, no layman is to farm the church or its tithes, no religious orders to receive church tithes from a layman, without the bishop's authority; monks are not to be resident in parish churches; vicars in churches appropriate are to have proper maintenance. Spelman, ii. 101, 122, 128.

The monasteries in England, restored by Edgar and Dunstan, had not escaped the evils of the times. "Monks," says the contemporary historian, "differed little in their lives and conversation from secular men. They kept not to their habit or their vows, but indulged in many vices. Their order, brought back at the instigation of William to its primitive discipline, and restored to its pious customs, now became greatly respected. New abbots were appointed by the king; and many monks educated in French monasteries, placed over the English by the king's command, established discipline among them, and set them a pattern of religious life."[6] Everywhere abbeys and priories rose with greater splendour and magnificence, and once more totally eclipsed, in the estimation of the rich and the noble, the old parish churches. The learning of the monk, his piety, his asceticism, his charity to the poor, seemed to point him out as specially deserving the contributions and gifts of the devout, and as better qualified than any other to turn these gifts to good account. So the great lay lords bestowed the churches and tithes in their possession on the religious houses, as more competent than themselves to

---

[6] Order. Vit., p 518.

exercise the duties of the patron, and watch over the interests of the parish church. Some gave two-thirds of their tithes, leaving one-third to the incumbent; some their chapels, others their cemeteries; some, as if these were too stinted proportions for their bounty, gave mills, fish-ponds, churches, church endowments,[7] tithes, all in one offering.[8]

Now in this transfer of their churches and endowments, it is quite clear that these lords were disposing of what was their own, and

---

[7] Order. Vit., p. 465.
[8] At the foundation of the Abbey of St. Evreux one great Norman family gave a church, with all the tithes and the priest's glebe-land, with arable land for three ploughs, a vill with the clerk's benefice, and a tithe of all the mills in the vill (village); also another vill with a monastery, its church, &c. Besides numerous similar benefactions, a tithe of wax and of Peter-pence, a fourth part of the monastery of St. Peter at Newmarket, a tithe of the moiety of the tolls of the whole vill and also of the mills.

In the year 1100, Harold the Lord of Ewyas gave to the abbey of St. Peter at Gloucester the church of St. Michael, with the chapel of St. Nicholas de Castro, the chapel of St. James of Ewyas, the chapel of St. Keane, &c. He gave besides a tenth of the produce of his hunting, of his honey, and of all things of which a Christian ought to pay tithes; also the church of Foy with one plough-land, the tithes of his fish-pond at Foy, the mill, the church of Sidred with all its appurtenances, the church of Abyngton, and the church of Burnham. He gave besides the tithe of all his demesne lands for the special use of the was not and never had been national property, or had been given to the Church by the nation in any way. They were, in fact, doing precisely the same as if a rich manufacturer at Manchester should build a chapel and then give it to the Methodists or any other body of dissenters; and it would be just as reasonable to call the one national as the other. Such instances as I have quoted above might be produced by hundreds, if the limits of my space would permit. But they are familiar to all readers of history; and those who wish for more need search no farther than the history of any one of the religious houses in England. In fact, nothing can be more futile, preposterous, and absurd, than the popular notion that the parochial tithes and endowments of the Church

---

convent, and a tithe of his mills and his eels. Hist. Monast. Gloucest. i. 76.

Once more: in the year 1134, Hugh, son of William the Norman, gave to the same abbey the church of St. David at Kylpec, with the chapel of St. Mary of the Castle, and all his churches and chapels, and the lands which belonged to them. He gave besides the tithes of wheat, hay, flax, wool, cheese, brood-mares, calves, lambs, sucking-pigs, and of all other things of which a Christian man ought to pay tithes. He granted besides that the pigs of the prior should go with his own to peasen and pannage (peas and mast), and besides the common use of his woods for their tenants. Ib. 91.

of England were given by the nation as such, and were not the private charities of individuals, as much, to all intents and purposes, as a subscription at a missionary sermon in a Baptist chapel, or a contribution at a Wesleyan Centenary.[9] These lords had a right to withhold or a right to give; but when they had given these tithes and endowments, and bound their estates for that purpose, their successors had no right to take them away; any more than they would now, in the case of any chapel or hospital whatever, without the consent of the owners. For a gift is as much the sole and exclusive property of the recipient as what he acquires by his own industry.

Nay, more: these transfers were made in the same way and with the same solemnity as religious collections are now made.[10] They were offered at the altar and dedicated to God's service. And here, in fact, was the injury to the parochial churches; the service of the abbey was more imposing, as that of our cathedrals now is; the plain and simple parochial church, with its single priest, could not

[9] [See Editor's note on Origin of Tithe, p. 151.]

[10] Sometimes by placing a knife or the key of the church on the altar in the presence of the whole convent (Chron. Abingd. ii. 19. 109); or by other material emblems of the transfer.

vie with the attractions of the monastic church. It had no such relics of saints, no such soul-moving and eloquent preachers, no such shrines, no such music. So, wherever it was possible, the rich and the noble frequented the abbey church, made their oblations there, left money for their obits and their anniversaries; whilst the poor and the bondmen, who had little or nothing to give, attended the parish church. And thus again the parochial clergy were neglected by the great and the wealthy.

Now, if in the transfer of churches and endowments, the monks had simply come into the place, and enjoyed no more than the rights, of the original patron, little harm would have been done; but then they would have received no benefit. At first they were contented to leave the incumbent in full possession of his benefice, accepting only a small annual pension.[1] If indeed the parish church was not far from the abbey it might be served by one of the monks,

---

[1] Thus in Battle Abbey the monks received an annuity of 10s. from the incumbents of the churches given them by the Conqueror. Afterwards the pension was increased to 40s. At last, not content with this they took the whole tithes and put in a vicar. Again, in some instances, they arranged with the incumbent that his son should succeed to the living on payment of a fine or of a larger pension. Chron. of Battle, p. 122. Chron. Abingd. ii. 28.

and the profits of the living be monopolized by the monastery.[2] But as no monk could permanently reside out of his cloister, nor discipline be maintained if he did, the attempt was soon abandoned. The next step was to augment the pension; and as land increased in value and cultivation, and the tithes became more prolific, the hardship to the parish priest was not so great as at first sight it might have appeared. And although this practice was a return to the old abuses of lay patronage condemned by the Church, yet as the monks spent their revenues in devotion, hospitality, and relief of the poor, and even ran themselves into debt mainly for these purposes, these pensions, though abstracted from the parochial churches, seemed liable to little objection. It is to these causes we must attribute the facility of the bishops and rulers of the Church in allowing and sometimes encouraging these proceedings. But as the expenses of the monks advanced with the augmentation of their numbers, the magnificence of

---

[2] In one instance, when a church in Suffolk was given to the monks of Abingdon by the lord of the manor, they seem to have served it in person and been recommended by the Archbishop to the Bishop of Norwich. Abingd. Chron. ii. 63. That also is Selden's opinion: "Some of the monks received into orders discharged the cure." On Tithes, p. 99.

their buildings, and the increasing price of provisions, they fell upon another expedient of turning the churches which they held to a more profitable account by becoming non-resident rectors, as well as patrons, leaving the service to be performed by irregular and often incompetent vicars, for a small and inadequate stipend. The abuse became so enormous that the bishops at last obtained a constitution ordaining that in all cases of appropriated churches, that is, churches appropriated to the use of the monks, a *perpetual* vicar should be appointed, who should be instituted by the bishop with a competent maintenance to be determined by the diocesan.[3]

The bishops took care that the provision for the vicars should be liberal. Thus, for the vicar of Aldynge, in Kent, appropriated to the canons of Tunbridge, it was arranged that he should have the offerings and perquisites of the altar, the small tithes, all the houses within the precincts,[4] the glebe, with other perquisites,

---

[3] See the Constitutions of Henry III. in Spelman's Con. ii. 139, quoted by Kennett in the Impropriations of Vicarages, p. 26.

[4] It must be remembered that in earlier times people had taken refuge within the cemeteries and church's precincts and built houses in them. And by the Anglo-Saxon laws the

the tithe sheaves and tithes of two adjoining farms, and a moiety of the meadow belonging to the church.[5] In another instance, the vicar was allowed all the small tithes, the offerings of the parish, a tithe of the hay in three different places, and the whole tithe in another, the tithe of certain mills, the tithe sheaf of the demesne of the church, of beans and peas in all land cultivated by the spade, and a seam of corn at Michaelmas from the rectors (i. e. the religious house). Further, he was to be free from all burthens, from providing books and ornaments, and also from repairing the chancel.[6] In another case, the vicar of Brinkley had the altar dues, the small tithes, all perquisites, tithes of the curtilages, the tithes of the fruit, legumes, and hay in Westroteringden, and for a manse, four acres of land, two seams of oats, and two of corn for his nag. He was to perform the usual obligations, and present to the prior and convent at Tunbridge, annually, at the feast of St. Mary Magdalen, two wax-candles of four pounds each.[7] Once more, the vicar of Chalk,

church and glebe of the parish priest possessed the right of sanctuary.
    [5] Thorpe's Regist. Roff. p. 145.
    [6] Ibid. p. 149.
    [7] Ibid. p. 203.

appropriated to the prior and chapter of Norwich Cathedral, was to have a suitable piece of ground for erecting a vicarage-house and its appurtenances, and 5*l.* for that purpose; he was exempted from providing books, &c., and repairing the chancel. He was allowed the tithes of rushes, lambs, wool, calves, sucking-pigs, geese, flax, hemp, mills, doves, faggots, eggs, fruit-trees, curtilages, trees, &c., and all personal and small tithes not assigned to the convent. He was to provide requisites for divine service, such as vestments, candles, &c., and have the books bound at his own cost.

It is clear then from these and other examples, that this institution of vicarages was an improvement on the former practice, and by these precautions the vicar's portion, especially when he was exempt from the obligation of repairing the church and from other burthens, was far from contemptible. But whilst it secured a more liberal maintenance for this class of the clergy, it seemed to sanction and even encourage the lay patrons in appropriating tithes and churches to monasteries, and to justify the latter in accepting them. The example spread rapidly in all directions, and thus the endowments of the parochial clergy were every year frittered away and diverted from their original purpose to secular colleges, chantries, military and religious orders, guilds, fraternities, and nunneries; —all of whom, under the pretext of being religious societies, appropriated and distributed the common treasure of the Church, as they called it.[8]

It might have been expected that the bishops would have resisted these practices so detrimental to the Church and to the efficiency of the parochial clergy. But whilst the bishops were powerless against an influential body of men supported by public opinion, and a reputation for holiness and works of charity, if ever they showed any inclination to oppose them, the monks had various means of overcoming opposition. Their wealth and their estates gave them influence with the powerful. They contrived to purchase the advowson often at a greater price than it was worth. They could offer inducements to lay patrons and rectors, or

[8] Of course there is no such thing as a "common treasure" of the Church. This false and unfounded notion, minted in early times for the purposes I have described, has come down to us and is often at the root of the popular misconception of the Church's endowments. No Church has any common fund, except the so-called Disestablished Church of Ireland. Each parish has its endowment for the sole benefit of the parish, which the Church may augment if it please, but cannot transfer or diminish. There could be no wiser provision.

H

give pensions to both in the monastery. Their society was the pleasantest, their parks and their gardens better kept than any others. Even now in all their ruins, there is nothing so fascinating to the imagination, so touching or sublime, as these ancient abbeys. What must they have been in their perfection and splendour, when all their walls and winding aisles and cloisters resounded with solemn music, with traditional psalmody and anthem that, like their architecture, had grown in beauty and perfection from year to year! Miles over miles the great abbey bells sounded in the ears of the peasantry for midnight, matins, noon, tierce, vespers, and compline. For five, ten, fifteen miles round, there were no such farms, fish-ponds, barns, mills, dovecots, and preserves as those of the great abbey. In every direction they had carried art, skill, order, and culture of every kind, based upon religious love and veneration, and not for profit or for sale. Such works seemed to all fit to be had in reverence and honour, worthy of encouragement even at the cost of what seemed humbler things; and he must have been more than usually hard-hearted and inexorable, who could think of offering opposition to any form of benevolence by which such works were to be promoted and sustained. So, partly from these causes, and partly from their influence with Rome, the monks had their own way, and set the authority of the bishops at defiance. The maintenance of the vicar was reduced or converted into specie payment, sometimes of five, sometimes of ten marks, which grew every year less adequate to his wants as his burthens increased and the value of money declined, until at last he was compelled to eke out a scanty livelihood by taking a chantry,[9] saying masses for the

[9] It is to this practice that Chaucer alludes in his affecting description of the poor Parson (the parochial clergyman), whose hard lot and conscientious performance of his duties touched the heart of the poet, as it did of many others, and formed such a contrast to the religious orders.

"He sette not his benefice to hire,
And left his sheep incomberd in the mire;
And ran to Londone, unto St. Poule's,
To seeken him a chaunterie for soules."

And in his brother the Ploughman (the small farmer) we have a picture of the class to which the parochial clergy belonged and of their parishioners:—

"A true swynker and a good was he,
Living in peace and parfait charitie.
God loved he best with all his truè heart
At allè times, though he gained or smart,
And then his neighbour right as himselve.
He would thresh, and thereto dike and delve
For Christés sake, with every porè wight
Withouten hire, if it lay in his might."

And he was as conscientious in paying his tithes as his brother was in the performance of his ministerial duties.

dead, or acting as middle-man and farmer to the "religious," or as steward to his lord, keeping his courts and collecting his rents, with all the odium attached to such ungenial occupations.[1]

Great was the evil, as might be expected, bringing the clergy into contempt, and providing a fertile theme of invective and remonstrance among writers before and after the Reformation. Convocation complained that the duties of piety and divine worship were neglected, the honour of the Church prostituted, the clerical functions despised, preaching and the cure of souls disregarded. Representations were addressed to the King and the Pope. "The land groaned," they said, "under the burthen of the 'religious' obtaining churches to their own use; by clandestine and indirect ways obtaining grants from the See Apostolic, in neglect and even contempt of the bishops."[2] The Commons remonstrated to Richard II., that notwithstanding all the prohibitions of the laws of the land, the "religious," through their favour with the Pope, "mischievously appropriated benefices having cure of souls,

---

[1] See the Remonstrance addressed to Henry V. by the University of Oxford, in Kennett's Impropriations, &c., p. 63.

[2] Kennett, ibid. p. 76.

and grievously threw down the houses and edifices of the same to the ground, and carried them all away, cruelly taking away and destroying divine service, hospitality, and other works of charity, which were accustomed to be done, in the said benefices, to the poor and maimed."[3] Throughout the fifteenth century, and up to the period of the Reformation, similar remonstrances continued to be addressed to the sovereign. But when the Lancastrians came to the throne, who before their accession to power had patronized Wicliffe, the most strenuous opponent of the religious orders, they found it necessary to propitiate such powerful bodies, and oppose all ecclesiastical reforms. In the weak reign of Henry VI., the abuse had grown to such an extent, that for want of sufficient endowment, "many vicarages were left without any officiating minister, whereby in many parishes, within the kingdom, weak men and women died without confession and other sacraments of Holy Church."[4] And thus it was that, at the period when Henry VIII. ascended the throne, nearly one-half of all the richest benefices in England had been

---

[3] Rolls of Parliament, 15 Ric. II.
[4] Rolls of Parliament, 10 Hen. VI.

engrossed by the monks—for they cared not for those that were poorly endowed. These fell into the hands of the king and his courtiers at the dissolution of the monasteries, with all their pensions and perquisites, and were entirely lost to the Church.

CHAPTER VI.

ENDOWMENTS AT THE REFORMATION AND SINCE.

THE poet Spenser, describing the progress of the Reformation under Henry VIII., in the allegory of Una and the Lion, singles out this spoliation of the parochial churches, as deserving of bitter censure. He, like all English poets, felt how great was the wrong thus done to a body of men to whom this nation was under infinite obligations for preserving and disseminating the truths of the Gospel among the poorer classes of the land.

> "He was, to weete, a stout and sturdy thiefe,[1]
> Wont to robbe churches of their ornaments,
> And poore men's boxes of their due reliefe,
> Which given was to them for good intents.
> The holy saints of their rich vestiments

[1] That is, the plunderer of churches, person'fied in Kirk Rapine.

> He did disrobe, when all men carelesse slept,
> And spoiled the priests of their habiliments.
> Whiles none the holy things in safety kept,
> Then he by cunning sleights in at the window crept.
>
> And all that he by right or wrong could find,
> Unto this house he brought, and did bestow
> Upon the daughter of this woman blind,
> Abessa, daughter of Corceca slow."[2]

By the dissolution of the monasteries, to which the poet refers, there fell into the king's hands 376 of the smaller houses, 645 of the greater, 90 colleges, 110 religious hospitals, 2374 chantries or free chapels, with all their revenues, movable property, money, plate, jewels, ornaments; and all the tithes, pensions, glebelands, of the parochial churches they had contrived to get into their own hands under various pretexts. By these means and by successive levies made upon the clergy, the revenue of the Crown was more than quadrupled.[3] Of course strictly speaking, and by rigid interpretation of the law, none of the monastic was Church property. It had been alienated from the Church, and was in the hands of the "religious" long before Henry came to the crown. The original lay patrons

---

[2] That is, the Abbeys, the offspring of Corceca or blind devotion. See Spenser's Faerie Queene, bk. i. canto iii. § 17.

[3] See Spelman's History of Sacrilege, p. 186, ed. 1698.

or possessors of the advowsons, were no longer to be found, and therefore, by the letter of the law, when the monasteries were dissolved, they and their estates were rightly vested in the king.[4] The Church strictly had no claim to them. But though they had been alienated from the Church, and were no longer Church property, it could not be denied that they had been often harshly if not unjustly engrossed by the religious orders, that the diversion of them from their original purpose had provoked loud cries of indignation. When therefore redress was easy, it seemed only reasonable and consistent that it should take effect. To what else than their poverty and the spoliation of their benefices, were to be attributed the ignorance and inefficiency of the clergy, their non-preaching and neglect of their spiritual functions? What but this was the cause of their servile occupations? What but their mean and wretched pittances compelled them to seek other modes of subsistence, to rent their own glebes and tithes, at such a price as their lords chose to impose? Yet now, falling in with the temper of the times, far from friendly

[4] The notion that Henry VIII. took away the property of the Church, or transferred it from one body to another, or set up a new Church, like many similar errors, has no foundation in fact. See p. 169.

to the clergy, the nobility and gentry of England readily consented to sacrifice the interests of the Church and the nation, by transferring unconditionally into the king's hands not only the monastic houses, lands and property, to which those houses had a just right, but the tithes also of the parochial churches, to which they had originally no just right.[1] With the exception of a few bishoprics erected by the king out of the spoils of the monastic property, the rest was reserved for his own use, or squandered away, or sold at inadequate prices to grasping favourites. So the Church was irretrievably deprived by the king and the parliament, as it had been by the monastic houses, of a large proportion of its original endowments, with the same result as has always attended similar confiscations, here and elsewhere—a total loss to the original possessors, and no advantage to the nation at large.

The condition of the vicars was not improved

---

[1] [Mr. Brewer must be understood to speak here of the *moral* wrong inflicted on the parochial clergy by the appropriation of the tithes which ought to have furnished their support, to monasteries, colleges, and other extra-parochial purposes. It is part of his case that the arbitrary appropriations and consecrations by the lords to the monasteries were legally valid; see pp. 89, 90, and 126.—L.T.D.]

by the change. Rather otherwise; with a recklessness and improvidence not to be explained, Henry VIII. squandered large portions of the monastic forfeitures like a basket of unripe fruit—not without the tacit persuasion that when all of it was spent, other sources remained. Large and valuable parcels of land to be obtained at inconsiderable prices, by a little court favour, stimulated the avarice of the nobility and gentry to purchase far beyond their means, and involved them in ruin which looked like the Nemesis of sacrilege. Money was not to be obtained except at high rates. Plunged deeply into debt, the new possessors had little to spare for pious and charitable uses. They pulled off the roofs of the priories and abbeys that fell into their hands, sold the materials to raise money, and left their impropriated parish churches to fall into greater neglect and ruin than before. The old hospitality, the doles of money, food and clothing to the poor, in which the religious houses had never been deficient, now ceased altogether. The vicars, deprived of those fees and offerings, which were numerous under the old religion, were now left entirely to their original stipend of five marks or ten marks, or 100 shillings. In some instances, when the whole impropriation was granted, that is to say, where no vicar had been provided, or at no fixed maintenance, the lay proprietor had the parish church served by a mean and insufficient stipendiary curate, at a remuneration wholly inadequate. In a report presented by the Archbishop to Queen Elizabeth, in answer to the House of Commons, it is stated, that there were in England 4500 benefices with cure of souls, which were not above 10*l.*, and most of them under 8*l.*, in the Book of the First Fruits.[e] In a petition made by the clergy to the Queen, in the same reign, it is urged that of 8800 and odd benefices, with cure of souls, there were not sixty sufficient for learned men. In a speech delivered by Sir Benjamin Rudyer, in the House of Commons, on a bill proposed for improving poor benefices,—but, as all will anticipate who know anything of these matters, never carried into effect,—the speaker went on to say: " I first moved, in the first year of the king (Charles I.), for the increase and enlarging of poor ministers' livings. I showed how necessary it was to be done; how shameful it was that it had been so long neglected. There was then, as now, many accusations on foot against scandalous ministers; I was bold to tell the House that there were

[e] Kennett, 168.

scandalous livings too, which were much the cause of the other—livings of five marks and five pounds a year;—that men of worth and good parts would not be muzzled up to such pittances. I declared also that to plant good ministers in good livings was the strongest and surest means to establish true religion : that it would prevail more against papistry than the making of new laws or executing of old; that it would counterwork Court contrivance and lukewarm accommodation; that though the calling of ministers be never so glorious within, yet outward poverty will bring contempt upon them, especially among those who measure men by the acre and weigh them by the pound, which indeed is the greatest part of men."[7] 6*l.*, 8*l.*, 12 marks, 12*l.*, 15*l.*, or 16*l.* at the most, seems to have been the general stipend allowed to the vicar.[8] Even as late as the reign of Queen Anne, in commenting on that Queen's Bounty Fund, Bishop Kennett, who had taken great interest in the inquiry, admits, that of 9000

[7] Printed by Kennett, from Henry Wharton's Collections, App. No. xi.

[8] See Kennett, who gives authoritative evidence for these statements, pp. 231. 280. 134. 279. 339. 231. 256. This author had access to bishop's registers and other sources of authentic information, which makes his evidence specially valuable.

benefices in England, nearly 7000 did not provide such a sufficiency for the minister as 100*l*. per annum.[9] Nay, the very fact of the establishment of this fund out of the First Fruits and Tenths of the Church—a papal usurpation in the first instance—and vested, like other spoliations, in Henry VIII. by his parliament, with far greater injustice to the clergy, and less plausible pretence than the monastic property—even this fund, I repeat, was an undeniable evidence of the lamentable condition into which many of the parochial clergy had fallen. For it is stated in the preamble of the Act, that, " Whereas, a sufficient settled provision for the clergy in many parts of this realm, *hath never yet been made*, by reason whereof divers mean and stipendiary preachers are in many places entertained to serve the cures and officiate there," her Majesty had been graciously pleased to remit the arrears of tenths due from the clergy, and suffer the whole revenue to be settled, " for a perpetual augmentation of the maintenance of the said clergy, in places where the same is not already sufficiently provided for." But this remission, confined at first in its operation to such rectories

[*] Kennett, 405.

or vicarages as were "of small value, not exceeding 30*l.* per annum," was not so munificent as it seems, for it was only granted, "as it now is, or shall become free from incumbrances," and no fund had ever been more misapplied or wasted, as a means of gratifying Court servants and sycophants.

Nor whilst the lay patrons and impropriators allowed the parish church to fall into ruins,[2] was it to be expected that they would feel any deeper concern for the vicar's residence or comfort. The careful observer of rural life in England will well remember, how within the last thirty years, the vicarage-house and garden were often little better than the cottage of an upper labourer, and the description of them found in the pages of the novelists of the last century can hardly be considered as exaggerated.

"Cannot a clergyman," says Archdeacon Eachard, reproving the hypocrisy of those who justified this mean provision for the clergy,

[2] "The Bishop of St. David's complains grievously (and not without cause) that many impropriators in those parts had either pulled down the chancels, or suffered them to fall, to the great debasing of their churches, and leaving them so open and cold, as that the people in those mountainous parts must endure a great deal of hardness, as well in the churches as in the way to them." Report by Laud to Charles I., quoted by Kennett, p. 216.

"cannot a clergyman choose rather to lie upon feathers than a hurdle, but he must be idle, soft and effeminate? May he not desire wholesome food and fresh drink unless he be a cheat, a hypocrite, and an impostor? Must he needs be void of all grace though he has a shilling in his purse after the rates be crossed, and full of pride and vanity, though his house stands not upon crutches, and though his chimney is to be seen a foot above the thatch? ... What a becoming thing it is for him that serves at the altar to fill the dung-cart in dry weather, and to heat the oven, and pick hemp in wet! And what a pleasant sight is it to see the man of God fetching up his single melancholy cow from a small rib of land that is scarce to be found without a guide? Or to be seated upon a soft and well grinded pouch of meal? Or to be planted upon a pannier with a pair of geese or turkies ... Let any man make it out to me, which way it is possible that a man shall be able to maintain perhaps eight or ten in his family, with 20*l.* or 30*l.* per annum, without a most intolerable dependence on his parish, and without committing himself to such vileness, as will, in all likelihood, render him contemptible to his people? Now, where the income is so pitifully small (which I'll assure you, is the portion of hundreds of the clergy of this nation), which way shall he manage it for the subsistence of himself and his family?"[3]

No one doubts, not even their bitterest enemies, that this nation has been, and is, indebted to the parochial clergy for their constant and invaluable services—services, without which all other national efforts in the cause of liberty, education, and good government, would have been barren and ineffectual. No one doubts that their ministrations among the poor, obscure and neglected classes of the realm, have made those classes loyal, obedient, and laborious subjects. Nor can any one doubt that in the clergy the poor have found their best friends and advisers for this life, as well as for the life to come. Their little social comforts, their penny banks, their coal and blanket clubs, relief in their sickness, advice in health;—of these and other blessings, the clergy have been the main authors and the indefatigable promoters. More than this, the influence of the clergy with the higher and the richer classes has continually brought to bear the better feelings and more effectual aid of the squire and the farmer in behalf of their

[3] Contempt of the Clergy, p. 77, ed. 1705.

less favoured fellow-men. To them this nation is indebted for the preservation and dissemination throughout the land not only of Christian faith, but of all those Christian charities, without which the land would be a howling wilderness. So patent are these facts, that they cannot be contradicted even by hireling orators or careless statesmen. Yet what has the nation done for those who, if matters be fairly weighed, have always been its greatest benefactors? At what moment of thoughtless generosity, into which men are sometimes betrayed, or of wise or unwise policy, has the bounty of the nation been directed towards those who most required or most deserved it? What Chancellor of the Exchequer ever provided a single item in his budget to meet their wants or extend and strengthen their exertions? If the imagination of this nation was formerly "fired [4]" by some generous and Godlike impulse, to set up and endow a great institution for "Christianizing all the people of the State," who can excuse its gross and extraordinary neglect in suffering the means it had provided for that purpose to be dissi-

---

[4] Mr. Miall's speech on Disestablishment, delivered in the House of Commons, May 9, 1871.

pated and wasted by monastic appropriations in the first instance, by the confiscation of those appropriations and revenues to the Crown afterwards, and by never insisting upon their restoration to its primitive intentions; and, lastly, by its allowing those intentions to be defeated by the niggardly maintenance of the parochial clergy, and doing nothing for their relief? But the nation may be acquitted of all such grand designs and such amiable weakness, for as neither at the first, so never afterwards, did this nation, in its corporate capacity, bestow endowments on the Church. Quite the reverse; both nation and rulers have ever shown themselves more willing to take than to bestow—and the grave irony of the naked facts sound like a sarcasm upon all such theories. For the Church has grown up by its own unassisted efforts, without any aids or endowments from the State. It had risen to its strength and greatness long before its establishment at the Reformation;—long before the increasing power of the monarchy enabled Henry VIII. to establish his Supremacy over the Church, in a way it never had been established before. No one, it is to be imagined, will suppose, that in thus asserting his Supremacy, Henry VIII. was also asserting for the Church new powers, or procuring for it new honours and emoluments. So far from this, his whole reign, after the death of Wolsey, was one perpetual endeavour to diminish its wealth and influence. In what condition he left it—and more especially its parochial clergy—let the following vivid description of a contemporary author tell:—

"Ye that be lords and burgesses of the Parliament House, I require of you, in the name of my poor brethren, that are Englishmen and members of Christ's body, that ye consider well this abuse (of inefficient maintenance) and see it amended. Whereas Anti-Christ of Rome durst openly, without any vizard, walk up and down throughout England, he had so great favour, these and his children .... that they had not only almost gotten all the best lands of England into their hands, but also the most part of all the best benefices, both of parsonages and vicarages, which were for the most part all impropred to them. ... If the parsonages were impropred the monks were bound to deal alms to the poor, and to keep hospitality. ... But now that all the abbeys with their lands, goods, and impropred parsonages be in temporal men's hands, I do not hear tell that one halfpenny worth of alms or any other profit cometh unto the people of those parishes. Your pretence of putting down abbeys was to amend that which was amiss in them. It was far amiss that a great part of the lands of the abbeys, which were given to bring up learned men that might be preachers, to keep hospitality, and give alms to the poor, should be spent upon a few superstitious monks, which gave not 40$l.$ in alms when they should have given 200$l.$ It was amiss that monks should have parsonages in their hands, and deal but the twentieth part thereof to the poor, and preached but once in the year to those that paid the tithes of the parsonages. It was amiss that they scarcely among twenty set one sufficient vicar to preach for the tithes that they received.

"But see, now, how that that was amiss is amended for all the godly pretence. It is amended even as the devil amended his dame's leg (as it is in the proverb), when he should have set it right, he brake it quite in pieces. The monks gave too little alms and set unable persons many times in their benefices. But now, where 20$l.$ was given yearly to the poor, in more than one hundred places in England, is not one meal's meat given; this is a fair amendment! Where they had always one or other vicar, that either preached, or hired some to preach, now there is no vicar at all, but the farmer is vicar and parson altogether, and only an old cast-a-way monk or friar, which can scarcely say his matins, is hired for twenty or thirty shillings, meat and drink; yea, in some places for meat and drink alone, without any wages. I know, and not I alone, but twenty thousand men know more than 500 vicarages and parsonages thus well and gospelly served!"[5]

[5] Roderick Mors (Henry Brinklow), quoted by Kennett from the Monasticon, p. 128.

The Statute 32 Hen. VIII, ch. 7, is sometimes referred to as indicating that monarch's love for the Church. That statute provides for the payment and recovery of tithes by conventing the offender before the Ordinary. But the Church's right and benefit were never intended by the Act or the Parliament that passed it. In the troubles arising at the Reformation tithes were frequently withheld, and the monastic impropriators did not or could not enforce their strict and regular payment. When their estates and impropriations were transferred to the king and to laymen, those from whom the tithes were due thought they would find as easy masters as the monks had been. From this cause, and partly, perhaps, from a feeling that tithes were not rightly due to lay impropriators, they were not forward in paying their tithes and oblations. The Act was a device to compel them by the shortest and most summary process; and thus the lay owners made use of the Church's power to secure for themselves the payment of that which, mainly speaking, belonged to the Church and not to themselves, defrauding the vicars of their

Edward VI added nothing to the revenues of the Church, but dissolved and annexed to the Crown the See of Durham, annihilated the See of Gloucester, and converted it into an exempt archdeaconry. He permitted at one time thirteen manors to be alienated from one bishopric, and thirty-four from another. By his Commission for removing shrines and church plate, the churches were stripped of all decent means for divine service; and as an historian tells us, "private men's halls were hung with altar cloths, their tables and beds covered with copes instead of carpets and coverlets. Many drank at their daily meals in chalices; and no wonder if, in proportion, it came to the share of their horses to be watered in rich coffins of marble."[6]

Of the reign of Mary I need say nothing. Her sister Elizabeth, though favourable to the Church of England, was too much imbued with the spirit of her father to enrich the clergy, and

---

just maintenance. This is clear from the wording of the Act, which speaks of "tithes and oblations commonly due to the owners, proprietaries and possessors of the parsonages, vicarages," &c.

[6] See Fuller, who cannot be suspected of exaggeration. Church Hist. iv. pp. 103, 104, and note; and p. 96, ed. Oxford, 1845.

perhaps too necessitous to spare money for alleviating their condition. So she abandoned the more generous intentions of her predecessor, who had given up her claim to first-fruits and tenths, and had passed a bill for restoring impropriations to their original purpose. A better era dawned under James I., who had "planted churches through all Scotland and the borders with 30*l.* a year apiece, with a house and glebe."[7] He proposed to do something of the kind for England, but his design was defeated. Charles I., a zealous churchman, was too much occupied by his own difficulties and necessities to carry out his wishes; and a suspicion of his intention to restore impropriations raised him up a host of enemies among the wealthy body of the laity. Under the Commonwealth the Church and the clergy were alike proscribed—forbidden to teach or minister, even in private, under the severest penalties, by men who had ever ringing on their lips the cry of religious equality. The Restoration of Charles II. replaced the clergy in their rightful possession, from which they had been ejected by the Presbyterians and stripped of

---

[7] See Rous's Speech in Kennett, Ap. p. 29. In fact, Scotland is the only country where the Church has been endowed by the State, first by James, and then by William III.

their revenues, but removed none of those evils of insufficient maintenance to which they were subjected; rather the reverse. William's good intentions evaporated in mere professions. Anne, as I have said, restored to the Church the First-fruits and Tenths, which ought never to have been taken away from it; and had never been applied by the Crown to national or religious purposes. What has been done since need not be told, for it is not pretended, even by the most violent opponents of Establishment, that the kings of the House of Hanover or their Parliaments have departed from the policy of their predecessors, or diverted to the Church any portion of the national revenue.[8]

[8] I have spoken of the Endowments of the National Church, not overlooking the fact that in the year 1711 the Commons passed a Bill for building fifty new churches in London and Westminster, and for that purpose gave the duty of one shilling a chaldron upon coals from 1716 to 1719, or rather transferred the duty, from the building of St. Paul's, to that purpose. But these churches *were not endowed*, nor can this Act in any degree be considered as a national endowment, as the duty was not levied on the nation, but on the inhabitants of London and Westminster, in whose behalf these new churches were erected. This was no more than a local act, enabling London and Westminster to do what they could not have done of themselves.

How then, it may be asked, has the Church been raised from the necessitous condition, so often alluded to in these pages, and its wants been more adequately relieved? For although the maintenance of the parochial clergy, and especially of the parochial curates, is still much below what it ought to be, it is in many respects far better than it was a century ago.[9] I answer that for this improvement the Church is not indebted to the State, but to its own exclusive efforts, and to the voluntary contributions of its lay and ecclesiastical members. From the days of Edward VI. until a very recent period, there have never been wanting bishops and beneficed clergymen of the Church of England, who have felt strongly the hardships of the parochial clergy, and devoted large sums of money to the improvement of their maintenance. Dr. Juxon augmented the incomes of thirty-two vicarages. Dr. Sheldon expended on the same and similar purposes 72,000*l*. Dr. Warner, Bishop of Rochester, besides devoting his income to free schools, the reparation of churches, and annual pensions to various parishes, left 2000*l*. for buying impropriations and improving poor vicar-

---

[9] The average income of the clergy does not amount to £300 a year.

ages. Dr. Thorndike gave his parsonage of Great Carlton and all his estates in Scamblesby for the same purpose. Their example was followed by Dr. Barrow, Dr. Gunning, Dr. Morley, and Archbishop Sancroft. Nor were the laity backward in this good work, resigning their impropriations, at no small sacrifice, for the augmentation of the vicarages.[1] " However despairing some may be," says Dr. Eachard, " yet I must confess it rejoices my heart more than a little to call to mind how the bishops have augmented the vicarages in their gifts; and to hear of several sums of money now employed towards the redeeming of the great tithes; and to understand that there be many well-disposed people that have already given back their impropriations to the Church, and that there be others that have made such purchases on purpose so to settle them afterward."[2] These words were written at the close of the seventeenth century. What has been done since then scarcely requires comment; nor need I insist on the energetic efforts made by the Established Church to remove from itself all reproach, and make full

---

[1] Bishop Kennett has collected various instances with great care, from the Prerogative Office and elsewhere.

[2] Some Observations, &c., p. 72, ed. 1705.

proof of its ministry. Its various funds, raised exclusively by the voluntary contributions of its members, for building new churches, for propagating the Gospel in foreign parts, for improving the condition of its clergy, for providing for their widows and orphans, for the relief and education of the poor, for the promotion, in short, of every good work, are greater, more exemplary, more munificent, than any other nation exhibits or ever has exhibited, or anything like it. They are a permanent monument to the vitality and energy of the Church of England.

> "As some tall cliff that lifts its awful form,
> Sweeps from the vale and midway leaves the storm,
> Though round its breast the rolling clouds are spread,
> Eternal sunshine settles on its head."

But so far as its churches and its endowments are concerned, whether before the Reformation or since, previous to its establishment by Henry VIII. or subsequently, the Church of England owes no more to the State than the dissenter owes. It owes the right of building its own churches and supporting its own ministers—that and no more. It owes the privilege of receiving the alms, oblations, subscriptions, and endowments of those who are willing to give them—that and no more. It owes its right to its own tithes to the same source and no other. And like the dissenter, like every other individual and every other society and corporation in the nation, it owes to the State the protection of its own property. That, and that alone is the one gift, the only endowment—if endowment it can be called—for which the Church is indebted to the State; that and nothing more.

CHAPTER VII.

CONCLUSION.

I HAVE shown then by a careful and minute examination of its history that the endowments of the Church of England, whether in the shape of tithes, churches, or glebe-lands, were not derived from the State, but were the voluntary offerings of its members. I have shown that the parochial tithes, to which the bishops surrendered all claim—and to which they now owe no part of their maintenance—were a charge made on their own estates by the landlords of England, in order to secure the services of a resident minister;—a voluntary charge they might have forborne, but having made, they and their successors were bound to fulfil, like any other contract. Whereas at first they might have withheld their tithes, and settled them elsewhere, as they did in bestowing them on the monasteries—

a clear proof they could not be national—custom as in other instances, obtained the force of law, as it does now, and customary tithes became legally appropriated to certain churches. The endowments thus held by the Church rest on longer prescription and stronger sanctions than any other property whatever; and we have a right to ask by what justice, and on what grounds, is the Church singled out for spoliation? By what equity is the Church alone to be deprived of its property, and all other bodies exempted? Where can be the worth, where the justice of that law which marks out for its victim one body of men and lets all the rest go free? But the injustice in this case is all the more because it is not pretended that these endowments are diverted from their original purpose. It is not pretended even by the bitterest enemies of the Church that its revenues are wasted in vice or in luxury, in fomenting schemes of ambition, in menacing the peace of the State or the public safety. If property could be lodged in any hands for the good of others, for the wisest, the most important, the most sacred of all purposes; if the strongest security could be found for the general administration of any property to the public advantage, where better could we look for it than in the clergy of the Church of England? They live in the sight of all men—their whole conduct, in the pulpit and out of it, is narrowly watched and scrutinized—the disposal of their alms and of the charity confided to their care, is hidden from no one. Taken from the middle classes of society, they are equally removed from the luxuries of the rich and the sordidness and temptations of the poor. Admit that in so large a body of men there are instances of human frailty and human infirmity: will these be extinguished if the clergy are deprived of their endowments, or compelled through their scantiness to find a livelihood less suitable to their callings? Or when the Church can no longer maintain its ministers, will it command the services of educated men or escape those evils it had to deplore when its clergy were no better paid than grooms or day-labourers?

Or is it pretended that the condition of our population is such, and such the state of religion amongst us, that we no longer require an active and efficient clergy? Do the poor need less than they did the consolations and warnings of the Gospel? Are the rich less exposed to dissipation and temptation? Or when the revenues of the Church have been confiscated, is it imagined that the noble, the rich, and the learned will drag religion out of the meanness and poverty to which it will have been reduced? Will they voluntarily honour that which in their political capacity they have dishonoured and degraded? If so, what can be more idle, unwise, or preposterous, than to pull down endowments with the hope of creating endowments? What more imprudent than to part with a good we have in expectation of no greater good to come? The arguments employed for disendowment are as devoid of all ordinary prudence as they are devoid of justice and generosity. They are such as no man could act upon in the ordinary business of life without ruin and dishonour.

On a calm review of the entire question, it will be admitted that no valid argument for disendowment has yet been adduced. If it be asserted that the Church is a wealthy body, it ought to be considered whether its wealth is out of proportion to the services it performs and the ministers it employs. If poverty renders a Church more holy and more effective, why is it not proposed to extend its advantages to other religious bodies? Why confine it to the Church merely? If these endowments are to be confiscated because they are national, they are in no other sense national than as all property, whether of churchmen or dissenters, is national; for they were not given by the nation, in the first instance, nor augmented by it since. But even if it were so, property once given by the nation ceases to be national, and becomes as much the property of the recipient as that which he has inherited, or acquired by his own labour. The nation has parted with its right, and can no more resume that right, honestly and justly, than it can take the property of any individual or any society whatever—that, for instance, of St. Thomas's Hospital, unless extreme necessity requires it, or the safety of the nation demands it; and that is not pretended in this instance.

It is not therefore on the supposition that the nation has conferred its endowments on the Church, it is not on this ground alone, that it would be justified in resuming them—for such a notion is subversive of all justice and of all society—but upon the same ground as that by which it may resume all property however acquired, viz. that it is employed to the detriment of the State. Nothing less than this—not even the presumption of a greater good. For if this once be admitted, the State would then have a right to insist perpetually on the redistribution of the property of its members, and not of Churches only, whenever the fancy took it that such property might be more wisely employed than it is at present. It would have a right to determine how much every member of the community should possess, and take away the supposed superfluity gained by superior forethought, industry, temperance, skill, and perseverance, and bestow it on those who possess none of those qualifications. It would result in making no distinction between the good citizen and the bad, between industry and waste, between all those virtues on which society depends for its welfare, and all those vices which are destructive of it. For the rewards of superior skill, industry, and perseverance, are as much the result of natural laws, ordained by God Himself, as the satisfaction which follows on a virtuous action is a mark of His approbation, and the remorse consequent upon vice is an index of His condemnation. And no State could exist for any length of time which should set itself to work to counteract these immutable laws. If, then, the assumption of tithes and endowments by the State were justifiable, it is not on the ground of its abstract right to interfere with the distribution of property,—for that right must be exercised in conformity with the immutable laws for which society exists, of which security of property is one;—nor because this species of endowment was a national gift,—for the donor has no claim whatever over that which he has given away—but because the retention of tithes by the Church is notoriously and confessedly injurious to the State.

This, and nothing less. For the property which every man possesses, whether in his individual or corporate capacity,—the management and the distribution of it,—are so intimately connected with his individual freedom, that there could be no freedom without them. There could not be any form of slavery more galling, and in the event, like all slavery, more debasing, than that which should capriciously interfere with every man's private property, or that of any company or corporation in the land; not because justice or necessity required it, but in the exercise of an abstract right. Whenever therefore a government contemplates such a step the necessity for it ought to be apparent. It ought to be a step which no government should take without extreme reluctance; not indeed in the supposed exercise of an abstract right, but as a last resource when all other tentatives have failed; as a compulsory violation of the very charter on which all national society is founded, and on which all national piety depends. Even if it could be plainly shown that the endowments of the Church are not so perfectly employed as in theory they might be—or so equitably distributed—and what human institution is exempt from imperfection? no wise and cautious legislature, tender of its duty and of the vast interests committed to its charge, would for that reason think itself justified in sweeping away endowments, and interfere with the distribution of property confirmed by more than a thousand years of national consent and approval, devoted to the noblest of all purposes, and intimately connected by a thousand ramifications with the rights of every individual and every parish in England.

CHAPTER VIII.

Supplementary.

FURTHER ACCOUNT OF THE ORIGIN OF PAROCHIAL ENDOWMENTS.

The account of the origin of parochial endowments in Chap. V (p. 77) taken from Bishop Kennett, and adopted by most antiquarians, may be accepted as sufficiently accurate for popular purposes; but for those who desire more minute information, the following observations on this very obscure and intricate subject may not be unacceptable.

As I have stated, by the old ecclesiastical theory adopted in this country and elsewhere, the bishop was regarded as the lord paramount of his diocese (*parochia*) or parish, as it was then called, and continued to be called as late as the eleventh century, long after the word had been extended to *parish* in the modern acceptation of the term. To him all tithes and endowments belonged, and his exclusive right to dispose of them was admitted, even after the Norman Conquest. From the earliest times it was usual to divide the tithes into four parts;

ORIGIN OF PAROCHIAL ENDOWMENTS. 135

and though this has sometimes been doubted, there can be no question that such quadripartite division prevailed in England. For in his answer given to St. Augustine, mentioned above at p. 38, when Pope Gregory referred to this distribution of the tithes as "the practice of the Apostolic See," he meant that this was the custom of the Romish Church; and wherever the discipline of the Romish Church prevailed, as it did here, and in the Carlovingian Empire, tithes and oblations were divided into four parts. So in a capitulary, dated A.D. 856, we find this statement: "Tithes are God's rent; by the Canons of Toledo, a third part belongs to the bishops, but we are content with a fourth part, according to the Roman usage." (Perz. p. 440.)[1] So long as Christianity was gathered up in cities, and extended only to a little distance beyond the walls, this arrangement was sufficient. The bishop resided in the central church of the province, surrounded by his clergy, and, as the area of Christianity increased, he sent out his clergy to collect the alms of the faithful, to

[1] This fourth part was secured to the bishop by a council held as late as 1120. See Hard. Con. p. 1979. Notices of this quadripartite division will be found in the Capit. of Greg. II. in A.D. 731; and in the Carlov. Cap. for the years 799, 829, 851, 874; again in A.D. 1000 in Schannat's Con. Germ. iii. 8 and Hard. vi. 787. [See note p. 156.]

watch the penitents, to give elementary instruction,[2] and, in case of necessity only, to administer baptism. For baptism in general could only be administered at Easter and Pentecost, in the chief church of the diocese, where a baptistery existed; and was not complete without chrism, which the bishop always reserved in his own hands. Preaching was exclusively an episcopal ordinance; and the canons strictly enjoin that the priest shall not go beyond his instructions. This then would be the condition of the Church in its earlier stage: the city, with its chief church, bishop and resident clergy; outside the city, Christian congregations visited by perambulating priests, and once a year, at least, enjoying the presence of the bishop. But besides these, there would be, outside the walls, a public cemetery and chapel, where service and the rites of sepulture were performed, and monasteries with churches, to which admission was granted to the male population of the surrounding district, and even the female, on certain conditions. Further, these religious houses enjoyed the right of sepulture within their precincts, a privilege of no small importance, eagerly coveted by kings, nobles,

---

[2] That is, the Lord's Prayer and the Apostles' Creed.

and prelates.³ As these monastic churches had no baptistery, and no monk was permitted to reside permanently out of his cloister, no monk could act as a parish priest. In fact, the attempt was strictly forbidden by the Church, and whenever the contrary happened, it must be considered as rare and exceptional.⁴

The obvious policy of confining the same missionary priest to the same circuit, the necessity of providing suitable places for receiving and hearing the bishop at his visitation,⁵ the rapid growth of Christian converts, would soon point out the advantage of some stationary building where the priest and his congregation might assemble for instruction, whether a private house, or a church constructed of such common materials as were generally at hand. And these, again, would be erected not in the country generally where paganism chiefly prevailed, and

³ It is ordained by the Council of Triburia, A.D. 892, that all persons shall be buried in the cemetery belonging to the cathedral church, or in a monastic cemetery, or in the cemetery of the church to which they pay their tithes. Sec. 15.

⁴ See Capit. A.D. 799, p. 79; A.D. 802, p. 107; also the Councils for A.D. 1074 and 1100 in Hard. p. 1519, 1859.

⁵ Thus in A.D. 747, bishops are commanded to visit their dioceses once a year, to preach to the people, "assembling them *ad competentia loca,* as they seldom hear the word of God." Boniface ad Cuth. Spelm. i. 238, 246. A similar order is repeated by the Papal Legates in England, A.D. 787.

converts were few, but in the more populous villages or towns, then little distinguished from each other.[6] No erection of a church could take place without the consent of the bishop, or, if it were parochial, without the relics of some saint,[7] a consecrated altar, and a baptistery;[8] and, if the right of sepulture was required, consecrated ground; for this would have interfered with the special rights of the cathedral church and cemetery. These rights were secured by the payment of the tithes and offerings made at the baptismal churches into the common fund of the diocese. In fact these churches became churches of ease to the mother or cathedral church, in the same way as they in their turn had chapels of ease when the parochial district became too extensive or too populous. These

[6] Baluze gives reasons for thinking that there was at first only one baptismal (parish) church in each city, town, or village. There might be other churches with districts, but they had no baptisteries. Note to Capit. ad Salz. p. 272. Migne.

[7] When this was dispensed with, the picture of the saint to whom the church was dedicated was painted on the walls.

[8] By a capitulary, dated A.D. 755, it is ordained that no public baptistery shall be permitted in any parish (parochia) except where the bishop to whom the parish belongs shall appoint. But in case of necessity the priest of that parish shall administer baptism. Perz. p. 25. The same order is repeated in A.D. 769.

churches are repeatedly called *baptismales, parochiales, plebes;* and they are strictly the ancient parochial churches, not the manorial, as is too often assumed.

The first notice that I find of them is in the earlier part of the eighth century; and as at this time canons and capitularies enjoin that no priest shall abandon his title (his cure) without leave of the bishop of the diocese, or perform service in any but consecrated places, or erect an altar in any church not consecrated by the bishop, or collect alms on his own account, or set up an independent altar,[9] we may, I think, justly attribute their commencement to this period. Not, indeed, that it is possible to assign a definite date in so obscure a matter, or that it is to be supposed that parish churches obtained at once the full privileges they now enjoy. Their progress was slow and uncertain, and they would only spring up and obtain first one right and then another, as necessity or the will of the diocesan required.

The districts assigned to these parochial churches were indefinite, and this alone is sufficient to show that their origin could not

---

[9] See the Concil. German. of Schannat, A.D. 744, p. 55; A.D. 745, p. 73; A.D. 747, p. 80; Hard. Concil. iii. 1889. Repeated, A.D. 789.

have been manorial, though it is not at all unlikely that pious laymen contributed to their erection and endowed them with lands. Tithes, of course, they could not give; nor was it needful, for the tithes and offerings belonged to the diocesan fund, and the priests of these churches were supported out of the fourth part, set aside for the maintenance of the clergy; and at later times, out of the third part, when the bishops, already sufficiently provided for by the lands and estates belonging to their sees, abandoned their claims upon the diocesan tithes. The emoluments of these parochial clergy were not inconsiderable, arising from lands and houses attached to their churches, and the right of sanctuary, which was extended to the churchyard, to the residence of the incumbent and its offices. By a capitulary, dated A.D. 785, it is ordained that every church shall have two manses and the right of asylum.[1] In fact, the cupidity of powerful lay lords had to be restrained from quartering their horses on the

---

[1] So in a Capitulary, dated A.D. 832, it is ordained that if there be an unendowed church, it shall be endowed with a manse and glebe, and two villani, by the freemen who frequent it, and if they refuse, it shall be pulled down. Perz. 360. And again, in A.D. 841, if a church be ruinous, the serfs belonging to such church shall give twenty days yearly to keep it in repair. Ib. 392.

parochial clergy, and compelling their *nativi* and *villani* to do the lord's work.

Nor was this usurpation of the laity the only peril to which the Church was exposed. Irregular priests and laymen, tempted by the material advantages to be derived from Christian piety and munificence, set up independent churches and altars, and diverted the alms and oblations to their own profit. Even the parochial priests themselves, adopting the example of lay beneficiaries, sought to make their benefices hereditary in many instances; or alienated the profits and endowments for the advantage of themselves or their families. The danger was obviated by various civil and ecclesiastical ordinances, invalidating all such contracts. It was enacted that no property acquired by a priest after his presentation to a benefice should be deemed hereditary, but belong to his church. The son of a priest was incapacitated from succeeding to his father's living, and the marriage of priests was altogether forbidden. When this proved ineffectual, the children of the priest were stigmatized by the canons as baseborn and made incapable of ordination.

Originally the limits of these diocesan parishes were undefined, as the purpose of them at first was simply to provide better accommodation for the growing necessities of the Christian converts, and ease the labours of the bishop and the cathedral clergy, many of whom were monastic. But in the year 823 it was ordered by a capitulary that every church should have the precise limits assigned of the vills from which it should take tithes; and this ordinance was repeated in A.D. 835.[2] The determination of these limits was by no means easy, and proved long after a fruitful subject of dispute. For as the whole social arrangement, not only in civil but ecclesiastical affairs, rested not so much upon law as upon prescription, these limits could only be decided by personal testimony, which was not always uniform. Such a practice, however, proved an effectual safeguard against forged charters and donations, in which the clergy are gratuitously supposed, by hosts of licentious theorists, to have liberally indulged. Charters were only secondary evidence at best, and their forgery was neither quite so easy, nor the detection of it so difficult, as is imagined.

The exact determination of these parochial boundaries became much more important when the question had to be decided on whom the burthen should fall of repairing the fabrics.

[2] Capit. Anseg. 532, ed. Migne, and Perz. p. 371. Like the manor in later times, a parish included one vill or more.

For as they were generally built of wood or other perishable materials, and the art of masonry was little understood, they were in constant need of reparation. The question was evidently one of considerable difficulty, and is often referred to; especially when, as we shall presently see, the rich and the noble, from one cause or another built chapels and oratories for themselves and their families, and withdrew their tithes and their offerings from the parochial church. In A.D. 829, the capitularies empower the bishop to order the restoration of a church destroyed by negligence. By another, dated A D. 841, all persons whose duty it is to pay tithes and repair the church, shall upon neglect be subject to excommunication. "Let the baptismal (parochial) churches be repaired according to the ancient custom," is repeated more than once.[3] Finally, it is determined that tithes and repairs are due to the parish church from all who have resorted to it for baptism and other rites. In short, the limits of the several parochial districts were not fixed by the extent of any one manor or territorial division, but by custom.

[3] Capit. A.D. 855, p. 634, and again at p. 438. No doubt the recurrent invasion of the Northmen gave an additional spur to these injunctions.

This custom was enforced by an ancient usage, which restricted to the bishop the consecration of chrism, and suffered it not to be administered except in baptismal or parochial churches. The ancient practice had been for every parish priest to receive it once a year from the hands of the bishop himself at his cathedral. When churches multiplied, and the absence of every priest from his benefice, at one and the same time, occasioned inconvenience, it was ordained by a capitulary, dated A.D. 817, that a certain number should be delegated for that purpose. "Of the presbyters who have been wont to visit the cities (cathedrals) on *Cœna Domini* (Holy Thursday) for the sake of receiving chrism, it has been appointed, that when they live at a distance one shall be sent, for every eight or ten, to the bishop, to receive the chrism and distribute it to the rest. But when they reside within four or five miles of the city they shall come and receive it as usual." In another capitulary, dated A.D. 850, it is enjoined that no presbyter in any town or vill shall administer chrism or reconcile penitents without the immediate sanction of the bishop. (Perz. 397.)

Such then was the origin of parochial churches. That in the troubles of the times, and the continual transfer of territory by invasion and political convulsion, they should often fall into the hands of the laity, and through the feebleness of the law be absorbed into their estates and regarded as their own hereditary property, was natural enough. Further, that the lay possessors claimed the right of patronage, usurped part of the profits, or let the churches to farm, reserving a rent or acknowledgment to themselves, is clear from the numerous capitularies and canons denouncing these abuses. Again and again the injunction appears, "No layman shall hold a baptismal church."[4] "If any layman attempt to derive profit from an endowed church the doors shall be closed, and the congregation deprived of communion."[5] "If any bishop lets a baptismal church to farm, the contract shall be invalid."[6] "No layman shall retain to his own use first-fruits, oblations, burial fees, eggs, trentals," &c. "No layman shall sell a church," &c.[7] "We see," says a capitulary of Charles the Bald, A.D. 844, "that the vengeance of God is imminent for the ravin and other detestable crimes of this age. Especially because the endowments of the Church, dedicated to God by kings and other Christians, for the

[4] Capit. A.D. 783. [5] Capit. A.D. 801.
[6] Capit. A.D. 823.
[7] Epist. Nich. II. in Harduin's Concil. vi. pp. 1035-1045.

sustentation of the ministers and the poor, the exercise of hospitality, the redemption of slaves, and the repair of His temples, are now diverted to secular uses. Hence many of God's ministers suffer from want of meat and drink and clothing, the poor do not receive their usual alms, strangers are neglected, captives are not redeemed, and the fair fame of all is injured. If these afflictions had been brought upon the Church by the pagans (the Northmen), patience would be our only remedy. Whereas we are oppressed by our own sons; by those whom we or our predecessors have begotten in Christ. . . . The laity entirely usurp certain consecrated places; of some they claim a moiety; of some they have divided the lands and glebes into various portions (for their families), and made them hereditary." (Perz, 385.)[8]

But it is time that I should turn to another aspect of the subject. Although the whole tithes and offerings of the diocese belonged originally to the common fund under the control of the

[8] This went on as late as the close of the twelfth century. For in the Gregorian Decretals, it is stated, that the patrons of parish churches took the revenues, and left so small a portion to the minister, that he was unable to subsist. In some instances he had only one-fourth of the fourth part of the tithes allowed him, consequently no priest with any learning would serve the cure. Dec. Greg. p. 150, ed. 1648.

bishop, an exception was made in favour of lands newly reclaimed; and these must have become extensive in process of time. Thus, in A.D. 816, Louis the Pious ordained that besides their endowment—for no church could be consecrated without an endowment—the tithes [9] should be exclusively appropriated to new churches built on new lands. At a Council held at Triburia, A.D. 892, it was enacted, that "if any one repaired a ruin in a wood (unreclaimed land) and built a church, by consent of the bishop, he might appoint a priest to it, with the bishop's leave, and give his new tithe to the new church;" in other words, erect a new parish. Of course, in these instances, the patronage was exclusively in the founder. In some cases the laity, to avoid the payment of tithes, engaged priests to celebrate mass in their private abodes; but this was strictly forbidden.[1] In other instances, they built chapels on their own estates, and appointed their own ministers; but as such chapels had no baptistery or cemetery, the tithes were still due to the parochial church, though frequent efforts were made to divert them. "Tithes," says a capitulary dated A.D. 803, "must altogether be given where the

[9] Repeated in the following year.
[1] See the Capit. for A.D. 789, 851, 876.

baptismal church was erected anciently, and devotion be paid there, as the bishop ordains. ..... But if any one wishes to build a church on his own property, with the consent of the bishop of the diocese, let him have leave so to do. But care must be taken that the more ancient (baptismal) churches shall not be deprived of their rights, and the tithes shall always be paid to the more ancient foundation." This restriction is frequently repeated,[2] showing of how little effect the law was to prevent the abuse of which it complained. "Certain of the laity," says one, dated A.D. 855, "especially the powerful and the noble, who ought zealously to frequent preaching, have churches (*basilicæ*) near their own houses, in which they hear divine service, and seldom come to the parochial (*majores*) churches. If the poor only come, what topic can the preacher insist upon except that they should take their afflictions patiently?..... Certain of the nobility and imperial barons entertain priests and clerks, without our licence —a privilege not conceded even to bishops— and permit them without examination to say mass in our parishes. This is altogether to be forbidden." And a little farther on: "The canons enjoin that all tithes shall be distributed

[2] See the Capit. for the years A.D. 851, 869, 875, 887, 898.

at the discretion of the bishop. But some of the laity who have their own churches, on their hereditary or beneficiary estates, dispute the orders of the bishop, and do not give their tithes to the churches where they have baptism, preaching, confirmation, and the other sacraments of Christ, but they assign them either to their own *basilicæ*, or to their own clerks, as they please." (Perz. 431, 432.) The result may be stated in the words of another capitulary, dated somewhat later: "Baptismal churches which have fallen into ruins, through the neglect of those who ought to have restored them, have gradually declined from their ancient state." (Perz. 438.) So parish churches just before and after the Conquest, both here and elsewhere, were ruinous and dilapidated—their tithes were diverted by the lay lords to their own chapels —their lands and endowments usurped—their clergy neglected, their congregations reduced to the poor cultivators and the serfs. Either they were converted into the manorial church, as the vills in which they stood passed by conquest into the hands of some powerful baron, or the manorial chapel usurped their tithes, endowments, and baptisteries, and took their place. So submitting to the influence of feudalism in other respects, they became generally ecclesiastical fiefs, acknowledging the ancient right of the bishop by the payment of synodals, and of the lord of the manor, or his steward, by a pension of various amount, afterwards made over to some monastic house, or dropped as insignificant. And this I take to be the real origin of the pensions paid by incumbents to lay lords, bishops, monasteries, and colleges, of which such frequent mention is found in our ecclesiastical annals. This was the true origin of lay patronage before the Reformation. The vill, with its priest and parochial church, set the type of the manor, and not the reverse; and the lay lords obtained possession of the parochial churches with their tithes and endowments, or allowed them to fall into ruins, transferring their tithes, privileges, and endowments to churches and chapels of their own foundation. So much for the pious superstition of laymen, and their slavish obedience to clerical domination.

EDITOR'S NOTES.

I.

ORIGIN OF LEGAL RIGHT TO TITHE.

It must be borne in mind that Mr. Brewer, in his treatment of this subject, is combating the notion of a specific legislative assignment of tithes by the nation to the Church. With this point before his mind, he lays special stress upon the records which survive of individual dedications of tithes to particular abbeys and monasteries, as showing how largely the free will of the tithe-payer entered into the matter. He must not however be understood as maintaining that the payment of tithes throughout England is to be traced to a multitude of separate and distinct grants by individual landowners by which the whole land became charged with tithe. The special consecrations of which abundant records remain in the chartularies of various abbeys and monasteries can hardly be taken as typical instances of the creation of parochial tithes. In point of fact no grant of tithes to the parish in which they arise has, so far as I know, ever been found, although the production of such a grant has often been challenged (e. g. Dr. Priddeaux in his book on Tithes, 17). Moreover, if the true legal title to tithes lies in all cases in a specific grant by the owner of the land out of which they arise, it is difficult to understand how the liability of so much of the country (by far the larger part as has been brought under cultivation since the date when any such grant was possible, is made out. It is admitted by most of the writers on the subject (e. g. Coke, 2 Inst. 641; Selden, ch. xi. sec. 3. pp. 360, 361; and Review on chs. ix. to xiv. p. 488), and proved by facts, that from and after the beginning of the thirteenth century, tithes became payable to the parson of the parish where they arose by *common right*. Monasteries, abbeys, colleges, etc. claiming tithes had, on the other hand, to prove a *grant* or *prescription*. This difference, a very important one with reference to the point in hand, is clearly discernible in the old cases on tithes. Thus in 1328 the Bishop of Llandaff, being also parson of Newland in the Forest of Dean, petitioned the Crown for payment of tithe out of a Crown mine in the Forest. The Bishop pleaded that "the tithe is due of right, and that it hath been yielded before this time." The Crown admitted the claim, "whereas tithe ought to be given to God and Holy Church of everything yearly renewing, although it fully appears that no tithes have been heretofore given of such kind of profit." In other words, the Crown admitted the common right of the parson, although it repudiated the notion of grant or prescription. Again, to cite a case of appropriated tithes, in 1304 the Prior and Convent of Christchurch petitioned the Crown for the tithe of all coneys in the Crown manor of Thorle in the Isle of Wight, which the Convent claimed under a deed of grant to them of such tithe by Isabella de Fortibus, late Countess of Albemarle. In reply, the Crown directed the treasurer and certain barons to *inspect the deed* and do justice. The Convent, it will be observed, rested its case on a specific grant. I have given two instances, one of each sort, but many others will be found in vol. i. of Gwillim on Tithes. This divergence in the way in which the law came to regard *parochial* tithes and *appropriated* tithes suggests a corresponding difference in the method by which these two kinds of property sprang into existence. History certainly supports the same view.

It is impossible to say when the duty of setting apart a tenth of the increase of each man's land and labour was first taught in the Christian Church. Probably in the Apostolic age. We may at any rate take it as certain that, when the Gospel was brought to England by St. Augustine, this was one of the duties impressed by him on his converts and observed by them. As Christianity spread over the land, exercising an ever-increasing influence over the inhabitants and requiring largely increased means for the maintenance of its growing work, the disposition to ask and the willingness to give tithes would naturally become more marked. The Christian duty of tithe-paying was not likely to be underrated or forgotten by those for whose benefit the tithes were given. We may be quite sure as much as possible was made of the moral obligation to pay and of the evil results of non-payment. But the Church went no further than this at first. While all were exhorted to pay tithe, and the devout did so, those who refused broke no canon of the Church, and therefore incurred no ecclesiastical censure. It was not until the eighth century that the Church of England began to demand from her members what hitherto she had been content to receive as a free-will offering or not at all. The payment of tithes thus became not only a Christian duty but also a matter of Church law. We have seen (p. 73) that the Anglo-Saxon kings to some extent, how far it is perhaps impossible now to ascertain, lent themselves to the new demand, and seem to have given to some at least of the decrees of ecclesiastical synods the force and authority of Royal laws. What the direct result of these attempts to invest the Church with a legal right to tithes may have been is not known, but apparently it was not very considerable. The times were unsettled, and even the frequency with which the laws were repeated, and as it were re-enacted, is a significant comment on the manner of their reception. Selden, speaking of this "fullnesse of laws," parenthetically remarks, "howsoever they were little obeyed," Review on ch. viii. p. 481. But we can scarcely be wrong in assuming that these civil and ecclesiastical laws, although they may have had comparatively little weight as laws, were yet influential in confirming and extending the *custom* of tithe-paying, which under the interested care of the Church had for centuries been growing up.

It is in this that their real importance lies. The fact that the Church, with the awful powers she was supposed to possess over the destinies of men, demanded the consecration of a tenth to the service of God, and the additional fact that the State endorsed this demand, must have acted powerfully on men's minds even although disobedience was not visited with either excommunication or outlawry. Without therefore enquiring too nicely into the precise import of any particular law or the actual practice at any particular period, we may safely conclude that, under the pressure of events, the custom of tithe-paying was notwithstanding many drawbacks, growing and extending throughout the Saxon period. The Conquest, as Mr. Brewer shews, gave a great impetus to the tithe-system.

What was this custom? It was the dedication of a tenth of each man's increase to "God and Holy Church," but not necessarily to any particular priest or parish. Indeed the custom of paying tithes began to develop itself before there were any parishes in the modern sense of the word. The dedication was equally complete whether the tenth went to fill the coffers of some wealthy convent at a distance or to pay for the support of the poor priest near at hand. Therefore after parishes were formed, although it was obviously the most natural course to devote the tithes of the land in a parish to the support of the parson of that parish, it was not unusual, and practically it was not discountenanced by the authorities, that a landowner should hand over the whole or a defined part of his tithes to some monastery or convent, in perpetuity. This was called a consecration or appropriation. It could only be effected by an actual deed of grant or by a practice of payment of such long continuance as to create a title by prescription. In the absence of any consecration, the duty to pay tithes to the parson and the right of the parson to demand them were assumed without any special dedication.

The ease and frequency of consecrations and appropriations may perhaps account, to some extent, for the apparent hesitation on the part of the clergy in early times to use the laws for the purpose of compelling payment of their tithes. So long as these appropriations were allowed, it was useless to sue a man in respect of an obligation which he could determine whenever he chose. But as soon as appropriations were stopped by ecclesiastical authority, so that payment of the parson could not be evaded by payment to somebody else, we find the parson bringing his action or suit and enforcing his demand. The nature of his remedy varied in different circumstances. If his title to the tithe was denied he had to go to the Common Law Court, but if it was merely a case of non-payment, or "subtraction of tithe," the Ecclesiastical Court was the proper tribunal. This however was only a matter of arrangement by the State to prevent collision between the two sets of Courts. The *right* had become a part of the law of the land. This state of things was not reached until the beginning of the thirteenth century, by which time the custom of paying tithe had become so firmly established and so generally observed as to be indisputable, while the possibility of defrauding the parish by bestowing the tithe elsewhere was removed. The landowner was not only bound to pay tithe, but he was bound to pay it to the parson of his own parish. Thus the parochial right to tithes became established and settled as a *common right*, or, as Coke calls it, part of *lex terræ*.

The payment of tithes being once established as a matter of common right, it becomes unimportant to enquire for any specific dedication to the Church of the tithe, arising from any particular law. Tithe is due "of right" to the parson of a parish from all land in that parish, unless there can be proved an appropriation dating from the time when appropriations were valid. But it remains none the less true that the origin of tithes in England is to be found not in any law but in the free-will offerings of the people. The establishment of the right to tithe was only the legal expression of a custom in which the nation acquiesced. That custom began in the purely voluntary gifts of individuals; it grew in the manner and under the influences above described. No real compulsion, so far as we know, was used. It continued to grow, getting stronger and more established, until at last the universal consent of the nation turned this custom into a part of the common law of England. Thus it is true that it was the voluntary devotion of individuals, whose numbers, increasing age after age, at last comprised the whole nation, which conferred on the Church of England her tithes.—L.T.D.

II.
THE TRIPARTITE DIVISION OF TITHES.

The question whether a tripartite or quadripartite division of tithes ever prevailed in England does not admit of any very decisive answer. There is no doubt that in early times when there was personal tithe as well as tithe of increase, a practice of dividing the offerings of the faithful into defined shares existed, and was enjoined in Italy, France, Germany, Spain and elsewhere in the Western Church. The authorities quoted by Mr. Brewer in Ch. VIII, are all continental. As to England the evidence is extremely slender. In favour of quadripartite division there is nothing except Gregory's letter to St. Augustine, quoted in the text (p. 38). With regard to tripartition of tithes the documents quoted in support of it are (so far as I am aware) (1) a spurious passage in the Penitential of Abp. Theodore (668), see Stubbs' Councils, iii. 173 n, 203; (2) a so-called Canon of Abp. Egbert (743), which is really an ordinance of later date and of continental origin, (3) the so-called Canons of Ælfric at the close of the 10th century, which however are not canons but merely dicta or collected opinions of an expert; and (4) an alleged law of Ethelred (1013), see Wilkins' Anglo-Saxon Laws, p. 106 ; Thorpe, p. 146 (folio ed.), and Schmid, p. 244: it does not appear in the re-enactments and confirmations of laws by Ethelred's successors, a fact from which we may fairly infer that, even if genuine, the law was inoperative.

But the better opinion appears to be that the code of which it is a part is a private compilation or collection of points of Canon Law gathered indifferently from foreign and home sources, published tentatively and not recognised as possessing any legislative force. With this exception (if it be one) no English law as distinguished from ecclesiastical ordinance or opinion directs the division of tithe into thirds or fourths, or refers to the supposed right of the poor to a share. Selden (Tithes, vi. § iii. p. 83) seems to think that the system of thus dividing tithes came to an end about 500 years after Christ, that is before St. Augustine's arrival in England. Lyndwood (ob. 1446) in the Provinciale (pp. 52, 113, 133, ed. 1679) appears to negative, by implication, the notion of the clergy being legally bound to support the poor and repair the churches out of tithe. So far as I am aware in the long series of cases, commencing in very early times, where tithes have in one form or another been the subject of litigation, no trace of such a claim is to be found. On the whole it seems most probable that if tripartite or quadripartite division of tithes ever prevailed here it was in the first days of the Church of England while ecclesiastical institutions were in process of formation, when personal tithe was paid as well as tithe of increase, and before the custom of tithe paying had grown general. (Stubbs' Eng. Hist. i. 261.) It can hardly be denied that the custom which ripened into right and finally became part of English common law, was the right of the clergy to receive the tithe for their own benefit without any deduction. The question has been fully discussed by the late Archdeacon Hale of St. Paul's; see *Essay on the supposed existence of a quadripartite and tripartite division of tithes in England.* Parts i. and ii: 1832-33; 2nd edition, 1837: and also *Antiquity of the Church Rate System considered.* 1837.

L. T. D.

ENDOWMENTS AND ESTABLISHMENT.

Part II.

ESTABLISHMENT, ITS ORIGIN, HISTORY, AND EFFECTS.

AUTHOR'S PREFACE TO PART II.

VARIOUS theories have been put forth respecting establishment, from the days of Hooker to a recent period. Most of them are ingenious, many of them highly suggestive. Yet, if I may freely speak what I think, they have generally been deficient in not strictly regarding the facts of the case or the intentions of those to whom this nation is indebted for that connexion between the Church and the State which we call establishment. No one who has carefully studied the history of the Reformation will for a moment suppose that Henry VIII., in establishing the royal supremacy, was consciously guided by the consideration that he was claiming no higher authority than that "which we see to have been given always to all godly princes in Holy Scriptures by God Himself;" still less, that he regarded the Church and nation as one and the same body under different aspects. It is equally certain that he never contemplated an alliance between Church and State as of two equal and independent societies; or supposed that he was connecting religion with the State by "a State religious establishment," and thus consecrating it to the service of God, as Burke imagined.[1] Whatever truth there may be in these notions, however plausible and ingenious they may appear as abstract arguments in defence of establishment, or sufficient answers to those who object to it, they fail altogether in explaining its origin, history, and purpose. They assume reasons and motives for it which had no place in the minds of those who fought out at the Reformation the great question of the relation of the Church to the State, and placed it on that basis on which it has descended to us.

Establishment was a political necessity. At no period of its history has the Church of England been independent; for it has submitted either to the supremacy of the Pope or to the supremacy of the Crown. When the long struggle between the two came to a close by the establishment of the latter under Henry VIII., the supremacy of the Crown remained alone and unchallenged. It may

[1] "French Revolution," p. 226, ed. 1852.

seem to some that when Henry VIII. made this Church independent of the pope it would have been more generous, perhaps more pious, to have left it to itself, and not have claimed a spiritual headship over it scarcely less strict than that which he supplanted. But then it must be remembered that this would have been opposed to all the sentiments of the Reformers and to all the arguments they had urged in this great controversy. Nor would the Church, unaccustomed to independence, torn and divided by internal struggles, have derived any advantage from such unlimited freedom; whilst other considerations, wholly overlooked by most writers and most readers, show incontestably the benefit of that supremacy to the Church of England so often deplored and not less frequently misrepresented. But for that supremacy, and the personal interest of the sovereign in the maintenance of the Church by virtue of that headship, the Church of England would doubtless have shared the fate of the monasteries. Without the aid and protection of the monarch it could never have defended itself against the numerous schemes of spoliation insidiously put forth by ambitious and grasping innovators, who insinuated in the ears of needy and arbitrary rulers that the estates of the

Church offered the easiest means for recruiting an exhausted exchequer. How far these schemes did proceed under Edward VI., and even under Elizabeth; what heavy blows were levelled at the Church during these reigns; needs not now be told. To that supremacy the Church of England is indebted for the maintenance of its revenues under Henry VIII.; of its Prayer Book, ritual, and its hierarchy under Elizabeth. Whilst then, as I have said, establishment was not a cut-and-dried theory, or a magnificent ideal, but a necessity forced upon the nation, no calm observer of history can doubt that, under God, it has been the greatest safeguard to the Church of England.

And as establishment was a political necessity in the first instance, it is equally a political and social necessity now, unless, indeed, under the pretence of disestablishing it is proposed to confiscate the endowments of the Church of England. It was possible to disestablish the Irish Church, because the people of this country were persuaded that its revenues were superfluous, that its parochial clergy had few or no congregations, and therefore were enjoying the usufruct of endowments for which no adequate service was rendered. Unjust as it was, it was therefore easy to confiscate the local and parochial endowments of Ireland, intended for the religious instruction of its people, when this country had been persuaded that few or none could be found to listen to such instruction. But with the Church of England the case is wholly different. No one believes that its parochial clergy are deserted by their congregations, that they have no services to perform, or that in general they are paid too highly for their ministrations. Therefore plain and naked disendowment makes no way with the people of this country, nor will it until the enemies of Christianity shall have persuaded mankind that religion is a fable and religious instruction altogether a mistake — in other words, shall have emptied our churches and left the clergy nothing to do.

Until, then, the millennium of Atheism arrives, and with it the desolation of Atheism, there is no great fear that the Church of England will be despoiled of its endowments; and that being the case, there is as much likelihood of its being disestablished as there is that Mr. Miall and his friends will disestablish the solar system;—for this vulgar, plain, and obstinate reason:—The parochial endowments of the Church of England exist, as all will admit, not for the sole benefit of the clergy, nor yet of their lay congregations, but for the benefit of both; and both have their rights in this matter. If a dispute arises between them, neither can be judge, for no man and no body of men can be judge and party also. There must be some higher and more impartial tribunal. Before the Reformation, that ultimate tribunal was the pope, who, as the representative of the Universal Church, was supposed to interpret its laws, and whose decisions as the supreme authority were practically infallible—that is, they could not be over-ruled. Since the Reformation, that ultimate tribunal is the sovereign, in his own person and by his constituted courts. Supremacy must be lodged somewhere, and these, as the Church now stands, are the only alternatives.

October, 1873.

ESTABLISHMENT, ITS ORIGIN; HISTORY, AND EFFECTS.

CHAPTER I.

ERRONEOUS NOTIONS RESPECTING ESTABLISHMENT.

It is obvious, then, that whatever exclusive advantages establishment may be supposed to confer on the Church of England, those advantages do not consist in any national endowment, or in appropriating any portion of the public funds to the support of the National Church. Tithes are not national property, and never were; if by that it is meant that they were ever in the hands of the nation, as such, and were bestowed as a national gift upon the Church to secure its services for the people. It is a remarkable and noteworthy fact, that whereas the nation has to pay out of its national funds for whatever other services are rendered to it, be they by the army or the navy, by the great ministers of state or the law officers of the crown; be they for national education or any other purpose whatever; the undivided services of the Church of England, without which all others would be nugatory, are secured to the State gratuitously. For the religious instruction given by the clergy of the Church of England, for their guidance and care of the poorer classes, for their salutary influence on the noble and wealthy, for all those forms of charity in which the clergy are mainly instrumental, this nation contributes no funds whatever, and, as a nation, never has contributed. Therefore, to repeat what I have said, whatever supposed advantages the Church of England may derive from establishment, its endowments are not of that number.

Moreover, that endowment has nothing to do with establishment is clear from another consideration. Various religious bodies possess endowments, but are not therefore established. The Wesleyan Methodists, the Independents, the Roman Catholics, hold churches, chapels, funds, houses, colleges, all of which are endowments; but not one of these bodies is established. And if by establishment be meant that relation to the State into which the Church of England was brought by Henry VIII. at the Reformation—and, correctly speaking, it can mean nothing else—the Church of England possessed funds and endowments long before it was established. Therefore establishment does not involve endowment, and is not necessarily connected with it. It would be possible to disestablish the Church of England without taking away a shilling of its endowments. It would be possible, though not easy, to disendow it, and yet not disestablish it. The two things are totally different.

But here I must correct a notion existing in many minds, and zealously propagated by some, that though the endowments of the Church of England might not, in the first instance, spring from national benevolence, but from individual piety and charity, yet, at the Reformation, these endowments were transferred, by the Protestant sovereigns of this kingdom, from the Church of Rome to the Church of England. Now as there could be no such transfer of property without the national consent, or, at least, without consent of the party in whom that property was vested, I have a right to ask, Where are the records of such a proceeding? In what Act of Parliament are they to be found? By what historian of the time—even among the Roman Catholics themselves—are they mentioned? It is true that Henry VIII. was an arbitrary monarch; it is true that he bent parliaments, lawyers, and clergy to his will; but the fact that he was arbitrary and could do these things furnished the strongest reason why he should make use of legal forms, as he did, and throw the responsibility of his actions upon Parliament and his ministers, civil and ecclesiastical. Whatever might be his wishes, he was too cautious to suppress even a monastery, or take its property, without a formal surrender, duly sealed, engrossed, and recorded. Is it likely that he would take the whole property of the Church, as it stood in his days, and transfer it to another body of religious men without some formal process? Would the clergy, who disliked the change, have surrendered their endowments without a murmur? Would they have consented to be turned out of their livings unless some law had compelled them? Would it have been possible that this proceeding should have been going on all over England and no one have heard of it at the time, no notice of it be found in contemporary records and correspondence?

But then, again, we have to ask, Where was this new body to whom it is supposed that Henry transferred the endowments of the old

Church, and thus created the Church of England, as it is now by law established? Where were its bishops and rulers, its convocation or Church body, who could receive these grants and endowments, supposing even the king had been willing to give them? A fluctuating body of disconnected individuals, however pious and eminent, cannot receive endowments and national trusts unless they are incorporated. They must have some one person or more to represent them and act in their behalf; and such an incorporation cannot take place without an Act of Parliament. So we are again driven back to the question—Where are the records of this incorporation, and how was the property transferred to it? Arbitrary as Henry might be, much as he might dislike the old Church, he could not strip it of its endowments and transfer them to some more compliant religious body without a long and laborious process that must have been known to some of his subjects, had it ever taken place. He might confiscate its property, but scarcely even then without leaving some evidence of the deed; but to transfer that property to others, with all the needful modifications and conditions under which endowments are now held by the Church of England, would have been utterly impossible without many notices remaining of so intricate and laborious a proceeding.

But, I ask again, supposing such a body had existed at the Reformation, why should he desire or attempt such a transfer? Henry VIII., in all respects but one—the assertion, that is, of his royal supremacy—was a strenuous supporter and adherent of the old Church throughout his life. He was as little inclined to depart from its doctrines as he was to adopt the doctrines of the Protestant Reformers. His bishops were the bishops of the old Church, and never of any other; his convocation consisted of clergy who were members of the old Church, and never of any other. Nay, the Reformers themselves, such as Latimer, however they might inveigh against certain doctrines and ceremonies of the Church, were members of the old Church, and of no other. Therefore there was no rival body to whom Henry could have transferred the revenues and endowments of the elder Church. Those revenues remained in the same possession as before; they were not diverted, they were not modified. Revenues of the Church of England then, they continue to be part of the revenues of the Church of England now. The possessors of them have changed, but the revenues themselves remain in the same channel as before. As, then, neither at the first were they given by the nation to the Church, so neither at the Reformation were they transferred from the Roman Catholic to the Protestant Church.

Seeing, then, that endowment forms no necessary part of establishment, and that it is quite certain that whatever else establishment may have done for the Church of England it brought with it no endowment, but rather the reverse, the question again reverts, In what does establishment consist? If it does not contribute to the riches and emoluments of the Church, what does it do? Does it confer honours and distinctions on the Church which it withholds from other religious societies? Does it invest the Church with a power and authority not conceded to others? Does it compel men to submit to the commands of the Church, punishing them for their disobedience, and leaving all other religious societies to make their way, as best they can, by their own unassisted efforts? Does it, in short, by some one-sided preference, favour, or encouragement, exalt the Church of England to the disadvantage of dissenting congregations, thus promoting the efforts of the former and discouraging and thwarting the efforts of the latter? These are the charges generally brought against establishment by its opponents; and it is contended that such preference is an injury to Dissenters—that the nation exists for all alike, and ought not, therefore, to select one portion of its subjects, or one institution in the State as recipients of peculiar favours, exemptions, and privileges it withholds from others.

I shall not here examine minutely how far the principle is just on which all this reasoning is founded—viz. that a nation has no right to encourage any set of men among its subjects, or show a decided preference for any society, however beneficial it may conceive such a society to be in its operations, and however conducive to the welfare and prosperity of the whole. On what grounds such a principle as this is assumed I do not profess to understand; nor can I see why the State is precluded, any more than a dissenting society is precluded, from the right of adopting whatever measures it may deem most expedient for advancing its real interests. Supposing, for instance, that it is the object of society to secure for all the greatest amount of happiness, and that it thinks that religion and morality, loyalty and obedience, are amongst the most indispensable requisites for promoting this end, the State would not only have a right to do whatever was most fitting for securing this object, and to encourage and reward those who most advanced this end, but it would be bound so to do; and it would be neglecting its most solemn obligations if it did not. Supposing, then, that in the estimation of the nation an established Church was best calculated to make men temperate, honest, loyal, pious; in other words, to promote the greatest happiness and good of the greatest number; the State, so far from doing any injustice by establishing a Church and advancing its influence, would be doing no more than its duty, no more than what it conceived was the best means of securing the general good. And, in fact, to do otherwise would be gross injustice; for "to him who knoweth to do good and doeth it not, to him it is sin." For consider: if it could be made to appear to the satisfaction of the State that dissent was an instrument of good incomparably superior to all others, that it did more than any other body or institution in the land to increase the happiness of all, that more than any other it promoted the ends for which governments are established; then it would plainly be the duty of the State to encourage, reward, and foster dissent, and establish it, if such establishment promoted its efficiency. *Salus populi suprema lex;* and if that safety and well-being consisted in dissent, or were more highly advanced by it than by any other means, the supreme and over-ruling law of all government, to which all other laws, all other considerations, must be subordinate, would constrain the State to tender, strengthen, promote, and regulate dissent. It is not, therefore, in establishing the Church of England that the State has departed from its duty, much less has been guilty of injustice to any, but either, through failure of judgment, it has formed a wrong estimate of the services rendered by the Church, or has set up the wrong body. It is not establishment that is wrong or unjust, but the erroneous application of it. It is not that it thinks highly of the Church of England, loading it with favours and exclusive advantages—if, indeed, it does so by establishment—but that the Church of England does not deserve them, does not promote the well-being and happiness of the State, as the State gives it credit for doing. If the State may not distinguish and reward those who serve it best, it may not reward and distinguish any one. It must treat with the same indifference its most patriotic statesmen and generals and its most inefficient and unpatriotic. It must betray itself and its highest interest by teaching the just, the humane, the generous, to feel that in its sight they are no better deserving of its esteem and its confidence than the selfish and the worthless. This is in effect to put no difference between good and evil, to obliterate the very dictates of conscience, to act the very reverse of the way in which God acts. It is therefore utterly absurd and monstrous.

Clearly, then, governments have an indisputable right, nay, they lie under the most solemn obligations, to use all just means for promoting the objects for which governments exist. And if to establish a religious society, and to fence it with peculiar privileges, be one of those means, they have a right to do so How they are to exercise that right is another matter. Whether this body or that is more fitted for their purpose, or whether this or that form of establishment, or this or that privilege should be granted or withheld, are details requiring consideration. But the general principle remains the same; that general principle being this—that every government is bound to select the means, the instruments, and the men best suited for carrying out its purposes; and in making such selection, if it passes over others less fitted, as it believes, for its objects, it is guilty of no injustice. Supposing, then, that the State, by establishing the Church of England, did confer upon it peculiar privileges and favours which it did not confer upon dissenting bodies, there would be no injustice in this act, and no contravention of its duty, if only it believed that the Church of England was a great and important instrument in promoting the good government of the State. Still more if its judgment in this matter had been fortified by experience.

But this, of course, is assuming that establishment did confer and does confer certain privileges, honours, and jurisdiction upon the Church which it did not enjoy before it was established. If, then, the Church of England was established at the Reformation—for that it was "established by law" before the Reformation no Roman Catholic will allow, since he denounces establishment as slavery to the State—the question arises, What honours, authority, and privileges were conferred upon it by establishment which it did not possess before? Were, then, its powers and its dignities greater after establishment than before? That seems strange upon the very face of it.

For however opinions may vary as to the policy of Henry VIII. or of Elizabeth, in other matters, there is no doubt whatever that it was their determinate object to assert their own supremacy over the Church in a way it had never been asserted before, and in a way the Church was strongly inclined to resist. To suppose, then, that they would go about to defeat their own most cherished purposes by making the Church richer, stronger, and more exalted than they found it, is an absurdity so great as to carry its own refutation with it. Men of common sense and historians may form different estimates of the characters of these sovereigns, but no one will credit them with a desire to confer new honours, powers, and emoluments upon the Church. Therefore, if establishment commenced with the Reformation, as establishment brought with it no accession of endowments, neither did it bring with it any accession of that dignity and that authority which are thought to give the Church of England such an undue preponderance, and to constitute a just complaint against the State for establishing the Church.

But further, what are those distinctions, and what is that authority, which it is supposed are conferred by establishment upon the Church?

Is it the right of its bishops to sit in the House of Lords? Is it to have the decrees of its ecclesiastical courts confirmed by the laws of the realm? Is it security for its property by national regulation and interference? As to this last, what security for property does the Church or any Churchman enjoy that is not equally extended to Dissenters? Can the mob pull down a dissenting chapel with impunity? Will the law decline to interfere if funds given in trust to dissent are wasted or misapplied? Is the clergyman guarded to his pulpit by soldiers or policemen and the Dissenter left defenceless? Security for the person and property of Dissenters is as great and efficient as it is for Churchmen. Therefore this also has nothing to do with establishment; it is common to the unestablished Dissenter and to the established Churchman.

And the same remark will apply to the rest. If Henry VIII. or Queen Elizabeth, in establishing the Church, conferred upon it any privileges or authority it did not possess before, what were they and where is the record of them? Did either of these sovereigns send bishops to the House of Lords who had never been admitted there before? The bishops had sat in the House of Lords from time immemorial. Did either allow the Church to erect courts of law and fulminate decisions, make canons and constitutions as they had never done before? They found the Church in full possession of these courts and this authority. They found it exercising an authority even beyond the State, and they limited and diminished that authority as it never had been limited before. If to lop and prune a tree, if to dam up and contract the course of a river, be to erect a tree and make a river, then did Henry VIII. erect the Church of England; then did he confer authority on the Church and bestow on it ecclesiastical jurisdiction; but certainly not otherwise.

As, then, endowment forms no necessary part of establishment, and it is quite certain that the establishment of the Church of England brought with it no accession of honour, emolument, or authority, but rather the reverse; the question occurs, In what does establishment consist? This consideration I reserve for the next chapter.

CHAPTER II.

ESTABLISHMENT, WHAT IT IS AND IN WHAT IT CONSISTS.

WHAT, then, is establishment, and in what way does a Church that is established differ from one that is not established? The word is used in various ways; sometimes to set up that which did not exist before; sometimes to strengthen and stablish that which is set up; sometimes to set up that which has fallen down; and sometimes, and more properly, as in the question we are now discussing, the establishment by law of certain relations between the Church and the State. Thus in the assertion of his regal supremacy Henry VIII. and his parliaments established a certain authority over the action of the Church which had not been established before; which is not claimed by the Crown in reference to any religious society with the exception of the Church of England. Thus Henry established, by Parliament, his exclusive right to the appointment of bishops, to assemble and dissolve convocation, to limit its prerogatives, to refer all ecclesiastical causes to himself, as the final and supreme authority. Over other religious bodies, their ministrations and internal management, the sovereign claims no spiritual jurisdiction. For if causes relating to dissenting ministers and congregations are brought into the courts of the sovereign, they are decided simply as they involve a breach of contract; as temporal, that is, and not as spiritual causes. No court determines the modes of transubstantiation in the unestablished Church of Rome, as it determines in what sense a belief in the Real Presence is permitted by the formularies of the Church of England.[1]

Now in the first meaning of the word *establishment*, mentioned above, as establishing, constituting, or setting up that which did not exist before, or in the third meaning, of setting up that which had fallen down, no one who knows anything of the history of this country will contend that the Church was established by the State in either of these senses.

[1] We have a clear instance of this in the disestablished Church of Ireland; for whereas before it was disestablished it could assemble no synods nor alter its public services without the leave of the Crown or incurring a premunire, now it can do both. Yet to the temporal authority of the Crown it is no less subject than before.

As St. Augustine and his companions brought Christianity into this island without the invitation or aid of the State, so they planted the Christian Church here without the aid of the State or nation, as such. So, also, the Church grew up a powerful and independent body until the Reformation, not owing its origin or its support to the nation. So Henry VIII. found it at his accession, and his successors after him. Therefore, establishment does not mean setting up that which did not exist before; nor do *thoughtful* men, when they speak of the establishment of the Church by Henry VIII. and his parliaments, mean that the Church owes its creation or its existence to any such act.

Nor, indeed, did Henry VIII. or any of his parliaments, or his successors, arrogate to themselves such power or authority. They never claimed to have created the Church, or to have set it up on a new foundation, or to have established it in any sense of bringing it into being. They do not even use the word "establishment." But their language is uniform. In the statutes of Henry VIII. it is designated as the body spiritual, *usually* called "the English Church."[2] So the king styles himself,

[2] 24 Hen. VIII. c. 12.

"Supreme Head of the Church of England."[3] So again, "the Realm and Church of England;"[4] thus acknowledging in this, as in other instances, the distinct and independent existence of the Church and State as two bodies under one headship. So Edward VI., "Supreme Head of the Church of England and of Ireland." So in the Act of Uniformity, "this Church of England"—never the "established Church" or "the Church by law established," still less as set up and created or constituted by kings or parliaments. Such a thought nowhere occurs.[5]

Neither indeed can it be imagined that before the Reformation the Church had so fallen down and gone to decay that it needed the aid of kings and parliaments to set it up again, and establish it, in this sense. Rather it was too

[3] 26 Hen. VIII.   [4] 31 Hen. VIII. c. 14.
[5] Henry VIII. uses the expression "the king's English Church and congregation" as he uses the analogous expression "the king's laws ecclesiastical;" but that is only another form of asserting his supremacy; as he spoke of his parliaments, his courts, &c. In fact, the great standing-ground taken by himself and the Reformers was the separate, independent existence of the Church of England under its bishops and kings, upon which the papal supremacy was a *usurpation* of long standing. How could that be if Henry thought that he was constituting and constructing a new Church of England? He and his parliament looked upon the reformed not as the new, but as the *normal* condition of the Church of England, which Romanism had perverted.

strong, and controlled both kings and parliaments. And as no one talks of a church being "established by law" before the Reformation, well knowing that no such thing ever existed;— for by the "establishment of the Church," and by the expression, "the established Church," or "the Church as by law established," is meant, as established by Henry VIII. and his daughter Elizabeth at the Reformation;—we have only to consider what they did, and what changes the Church underwent at their hands, so that not being established before, it became established then. That establishment did not consist on their part, as I have already shown, in calling the Church of England into existence, in constituting as a Church that which was no Church before, in giving more money, or more honour or authority to the Church—for they did none of these things—but in bringing the Church into certain relations with the State in which it had not stood before. That is what they did in "establishing" the Church; an expression not used by themselves to designate their action in this respect, but applied to it afterwards, at a late and indefinite period,[6] when

[It is used in the Canons of 1604 and in Charles II's Act of Uniformity, 1662. I do not find it in earlier public documents. It was introduced into the Coronation Oath, at the Revolution, by 1 William & Mary, ch. 6. L. T. D.]

the controversies of the time had brought out
into greater prominence the legal status of the
National Church as opposed to the illegal
assemblies of Roman Catholics and Dissenters.
So far from thinking that they were erecting
the Church on a new foundation, or bringing it
under a new form of subjection, the Reformers
always proclaimed that they were asserting for
it its ancient freedom, restoring the old and
natural relationship between the Church and the
sovereign, corrupted and perverted by the successive usurpations of the Church of Rome. "The
body spiritual having power," say the statutes,[7]
"when any cause of the law Divine happened
to come in question, or of spiritual learning;
then it was declared, interpreted, and showed
by that part of the said body politic, called
the *Spiritualty*, now being usually called the
English Church, which always hath been reputed and also found of that sort, that both for
knowledge, integrity, and sufficiency of number,
it hath been always thought, and is also at this
hour, sufficient and meet of itself, without the
intermeddling of any exterior[8] person, or persons,

[7] 24 Hen. VIII. c. 12.
[8] [There is a draft of this Bill in the British Museum (Cotton MSS., Cleopatra E. vi. f. 185) with corrections and alterations in the handwriting of Henry VIII. From this manuscript it appears that the draftsman had used the word

to declare and determine all such doubts, and to administer all such offices and duties, as to their rooms spiritual doth appertain."

This, then, is the first particular in which establishment consists—that, namely, of securing the freedom of the Church of England, and its independence as a Church from all exterior jurisdiction. Its restoration to its pristine authority and pre-eminence as a national Church, or at least what the clergy and laity at that time, to the best of their judgment and ability, considered to be such, was the work of the Reformation. And as establishment set up no new Church, neither did it set up any new creeds or articles of faith. Neither did the sovereign nor his parliament—though he might take the initiative, and set on foot the machinery requisite for inaugurating ritual reforms—claim to interpose in matters of faith and doctrine; nor in the exercise of any purely spiritual function, such as the consecration of bishops, the ordination of ministers, or the administration of sacraments. Neither did Henry VIII, in the fullest plenitude of his power, challenge autho-

"other" and that the King struck it out and substituted the word "exterior." The effect of the change is to limit the application of the clause more completely to *foreign* interference. L. T. D.]

rity in any of these points; for he himself, in his letter to the Convocation of York, most clearly and explicitly lays down his own meaning, and explains the limits of his supremacy: "As to spiritual things, meaning by them the sacraments,[9] being by God ordained as instruments of efficacy and strength, whereby grace is of His infinite goodness conferred upon His people; forasmuch as they be no worldly nor temporal things, they have no worldly nor temporal head, but only Christ that did institute them, by whose ordinance they be ministered here by mortal men, elect, chosen, and ordered as God hath willed for that purpose, *who be the clergy;* who for the time they do that, and in that respect, *tanquam ministri versantur in his quæ hominum potestati non subjiciuntur. In quibus si male versantur, sine scandalo, Deum ultorem habent, si cum scandalo hominum cognitio et vindicta est;*" that is, in these their ministrations the clergy exercise functions which transcend all human authority; and if these functions are viciously or carelessly performed, but without overt scandal,

[9] It must be remembered that by the word sacrament here, the king meant—besides the two sacraments as we hold them—confirmation, penance, orders, matrimony, and extreme unction; in fact, the whole extent of clerical ministration.

they are answerable to God alone; but if with public scandal and offence, the cognizance and punishment of such offences rightly belong to men.

Now it was by virtue of the freedom and independence of the Church of England, thus claimed for it by Henry VIII and his successors, that it was enabled to enter upon those reforms in doctrine and discipline it could not have attempted before. So long as it or its kings admitted the papal supremacy, it could not without the pope's consent have removed any of those errors and corruptions which it felt were destroying its efficiency as a Church, and the purity of the faith with which it had been entrusted. But a Church which cannot reform itself cannot exercise its functions duly, and is in effect no Church. And this was the condition of the Church of England, as a mere dependency on Rome. Its whole national life and liberty of action were absorbed into that of Rome; its authority had departed; its hierarchy, its spiritual organization, its whole energy were paralyzed. In this sense then Henry VIII established the Church of England—by restoring its nationality and independence; by enabling it to inaugurate necessary reforms, to exercise its gifts without waiting on the consent of any other authority than that of its national and natural sovereign.

But it may be thought that this was no great advantage after all; that a freedom dependent on the will of the sovereign is not more real or precious than when it depends upon the pope; that a spiritual superior, like the pope, is a fitter ruler for the Church than a layman who can neither know nor care for its wants and its necessities. And perhaps there are some who would even prefer such a spiritual supremacy to that which exists among us at present, or at least think that, for the freedom of the Church to be complete, it should be left entirely to itself, without any control on the part of the State, as the Dissenters are left.

Now though it is not the purpose of this chapter to defend Establishment against all the charges that may be alleged against it, but rather to explain in what establishment consists, I will briefly notice these objections before I pass on. Nor shall I take refuge in the obvious reply, that as no human institution whatever is perfect, objections, however well founded, are not sufficient to condemn it or authorize us to change it, unless it can be shown that they are fatal to its efficiency. For objections unanswerable in theory may either disappear in practice, or be so neutralized by other influences as to be reduced to a minimum. Is it true, then, that for the activity, development, purity and spirituality of the Church of England, the supremacy of the sovereign has been less favourable than the supremacy of the pope? Has it made the Church less sensible of its duties than it was before? Are its exertions for the salvation of men and its missionary spirit less vigorous now than they were under the papal supremacy? Has it denied the creeds or articles of faith, or depraved the sacraments, or accepted doctrines at variance with the Gospel and the teaching of the fathers in primitive times? If none of these things can be alleged against it, then it cannot be said that it has suffered any evil by the exchange of the papal for the royal supremacy. On the other hand, it must be admitted that the natural sovereign is, in general, from clearer knowledge, from stronger interest and affection, better able to determine what is right and good for his people than an external one constantly liable to false impressions;—much more if that sovereign be, like our own, bound by the constitution to be a member of the Church of England,[1] to receive his consecration from its bishops, to be baptized,

---

[1] "Whosoever shall hereafter come to the possession of this Crown shall join in communion with the Church of England as by law established." 12 & 13 Will. III, c. 2. sec. 3.

confirmed, married, and taught the faith by its ministers; if, like our own, also, he rules not arbitrarily, but by the regulated, solemn procedure of constitutional methods and advisers in Church and State. For such methods, besides providing for the due administration of justice, offer, also, the strongest barrier to violent passions and sudden resentments, out of which most acts of tyranny and oppression arise. If the sovereign were ever so strongly inclined to insist on an unwise or unjust deed in Church or State, he could not easily effect his purpose unless he could bring others to the same mind as himself and trample down the restraints which a constitutional government, like our own, opposes to the outbreaks of rashness and cruelty. In this respect a constitutional monarchy has infinite advantages over any republican form of government; for the will of a monarch bent on injustice may be controlled without injuring the machinery of government, but the popular will cannot be so resisted, and if not humoured in its caprices, the more violent often in proportion as they are more unreasonable, it bursts through every obstacle and every constitutional check like a heady flood, and carries all before it. In this respect, not to mention others, the supremacy of the national sovereign, controlled by law and amenable to public opinion, is morally superior to that of any ecclesiastical supremacy from without, unless indeed popes are infallible.

But if it be said that this supremacy, though nominally lodged in the Crown, is in reality exercised by Parliament, or by the prime minister of the day as the representative of their authority,[2] how, I ask, are the inconveniences arising from such an arrangement, if inconveniences they are, to be avoided by any ecclesiastical polity that can be devised? They would be equally great whether the Church were disestablished or not. The fullest amount of ecclesiastical freedom and independence will

---

[2] [A great deal was made of this argument during the minority of Edward VI. Burnet (Hist. Ref., vol. ii. pt. I, p. 144, Ox. ed. 1829) says: "The Popish clergy began generally to have it spread among them, that though they had acknowledged the King's supremacy, yet they had never owned the council's supremacy. That the council could only see to the execution of the laws and orders that had been made, but could not make new ones; and that therefore the supremacy could not be exercised till the king, in whose person it was vested, came to be of age to consider of matters himself. Upon this the lawyers were consulted, who did unanimously resolve that the supremacy, being annexed to the regal dignity, was the same in a king under age when it was executed by the council that it was in a king at full age, and therefore, things ordered by the council now had the same authority in law that they could have when the king did act himself." L. T. D.]

not avail to save any Church from the control of the State, if the State is resolved to control it. The Dissenters may boast that they are free from the trammels of establishment; but that is not by reason of any special excellence or virtue in dissent, but because they have not hitherto been powerful or important enough to challenge the attention of the State like the Church of England. Not caring much what Dissenters (as such) do, not alarmed at the exercise of any power or influence they may be supposed to possess, the nation leaves the Dissenters to themselves; and, if the Church were weak and insignificant, it might be easily treated with the same indifference. But if dissent became powerful, if its authority proved a dangerous co-rival to the State, the State would take measures to restrain and control it;—that is to establish it, and determine the limits of its freedom of action. And no outcry for the independence of dissent and its congregations, no claim to religious liberty, would be of the least avail in preventing this result. For the State, or the sovereign, as the representative of the State, is and must be supreme; and when that supremacy is exerted it must command obedience, be it more or be it less; be it shown in allowing Dissenters liberty of action, so long as it does not deem it worth while to interfere with them, or in restraining that liberty of action, as in the case of the established Church; be it irregular and uncertain as in the case of an unestablished Church, or regular and determinate as in our own. In fact, as a regulated liberty is better than liberty subject at any time to interference, the establishment of the Church of England, that is to say, the regular action of the State, limited by certain constitutional checks and operating according to a fixed method, secures to us as much freedom as disestablishment would secure, and is far less liable to disquietude and interruption. For it must not be imagined that so important a body as the Church of England,—so intimately bound up with all our social habits, so necessary to our peace and our existence as a nation that even Dissenters, though professing to despise it, cannot leave it alone,—would by disestablishment escape the interference of the State, any more than it does now. To do that it must cease to be important. Established or disestablished, its operations would be called in question. Its rites, its discipline, its doctrines, would still be canvassed and discussed in the House of Commons. Its bishops would still be regarded as amenable to the State for the execution of their great trusts. Its clergy would still find the decisions of court and privy councils as stringent and as annoying as before. Whereas now, the very regularity of the action of the State, in regard to the Church, is a most important safeguard against the assumption and exercise on its part of any irregular authority. The Church knows precisely when, where, and how the State may step in and interpose; what form that interposition will take; how far it will extend; and the State knows equally well when it may legally and safely interpose to the good of the Church and of the nation at large, without endangering the tranquillity of either.

Thus far, then, I have shown in what establishment really consists, and how far in controlling the action of the Church it interferes with its liberty. I have shown that in thus controlling the liberty of the Church it has in reality secured for the Church as much liberty as it would enjoy if it were disestablished, so long as the Church possesses the influence and endowments it possesses at present.

Why the Church cannot be left entirely to its liberty I will explain in the next chapter; but before doing so I must refer to an objection common in the mouths of Dissenters and of some Churchmen, that the supremacy exercised by the sovereign, in ecclesiastical causes, is inconsistent with his character as a layman. In the first place, then, as stated already, the sovereigns of this country perform no merely spiritual act; they neither administer sacraments, nor consecrate bishops, nor engage in any ministerial function in their own persons, nor exercise any spiritual jurisdiction except through the agency of constitutional forms. "When we attribute to the Queen's Majesty the chief government . . . we give not our princes the ministering either of God's Word or of the Sacraments . . . but that only prerogative which we see to have been given always to all godly princes in Holy Scriptures by God Himself; that is, that they should rule *all* states and degrees committed to their charge by God, whether they be ecclesiastical or temporal, and restrain with the civil sword the stubborn and evil doers."[3] Kings are as much consecrated to their high office as popes or bishops are. The sovereign is never regarded by the constitution as a mere layman, but as a *mixta persona*, partly lay and partly spiritual.[4] He is anointed to his high calling, and the aid of the Holy Ghost is specially invoked in his behalf, that he may rule the people "committed

[3] Articles of Religion, XXXVII.
[4] [See however, p. 299. L.T.D.]

to his charge in wealth, peace, and godliness." Unless, therefore, it can be shown that ruling the clergy is inconsistent with such commission, and is hostile to the peace and godliness of the people, no sovereign can, with a safe conscience, decline the duties of his spiritual any more than he can of his temporal office. "As the state of the Church doth now stand," says Hooker, " till it be proved that some special law of Christ hath for ever annexed unto the clergy alone the power to make ecclesiastical laws, we are to hold it a thing most consonant with equity and reason that no ecclesiastical law be made in a Christian commonwealth without consent as well of the laity as of the clergy, but least of all without consent of the highest power.

" For of this thing no man doubteth, namely, that in all societies, companies, and corporations, what severally each shall be bound unto, it must be with all their assents ratified. Against all equity it were that a man should suffer detriment at the hands of man, for not observing that which he never did, either by himself or by others, mediately or immediately agree unto; much more that a king should constrain all others unto the strict observation of any such human ordinance as passeth without his own approbation. In this case, therefore, especially, that vulgar axiom is of force— *quod omnes tangit ab omnibus tractari et approbari debet.* . . . A law, be it civil or ecclesiastical, is as a public obligation, wherein seeing that the whole standeth charged, no reason it should pass without his privity and will whom principally the whole doth depend upon. '*Sicut laici jurisdictionem clericorum perturbare ita clerici jurisdictionem laicorum non debent imminuere,*' saith Innocent; 'as the laity should not hinder the clergy's jurisdiction, so neither is it reason that the laity's right should be abridged by the clergy.' But were it so that the clergy alone might give laws unto all the rest, forasmuch as every estate doth desire to enlarge the bounds of their own liberties, is it not easy to see how injurious this might prove unto men of other condition? Peace and justice are maintained by preserving unto every order their rights and by keeping all estates, as it were, on an even balance. Which thing is no better done than if the king, their common parent, whose care is presumed to extend most indifferently over all, do bear the chiefest sway in the making of laws which all must be ordered by.' [5]

[5] Eccl. Pol. iii. p. 404.

CHAPTER III.

THE NECESSITY OF ESTABLISHMENT.

ESTABLISHMENT, then, is necessary that the rights of all may be duly maintained, whether of the Church itself, or of the sovereign, or of the laity. For consider, in reference to the external polity of the Church and its relation to the State three methods only are possible: first, the supremacy of the clergy over the laity, as in the Church of Rome; next of the laity over the clergy, as among Dissenters; thirdly, the conservation of the rights of both by the supremacy of the Crown, as among ourselves. Now it will be apparent on the very face of the thing that this last method is the best and the wisest. For the inconveniences which must arise if the laity be supreme over the clergy are so great and so obvious, that I need not waste time in exposing them. Nor are the inconveniences of the opposite method much less, or even less fatal to the real welfare of both. For though it might seem right that in all matters affecting the spiritual good of mankind—their instruction in the faith, their admission to the privileges of the Church—the determination of these things should rest exclusively with the Church, who is to draw the precise line between that which is purely spiritual and that which is not? That has never yet been done, and was found wholly impracticable before the Reformation. Shall the decision on disputed points be left to the laity? It will not satisfy the clergy. Shall it be left to the clergy? Then all things are spiritual. Moreover, as each class must have its respective rights preserved, who shall decide when they are at variance? Not the clergy, for they are parties to the suit. Not the laity, for the same reason. Clearly, then, the supremacy in purely spiritual matters cannot rest with the clergy alone, or the laity alone, because neither can decide the exact limits of spiritual things, and with whomsoever that decision rests he becomes supreme in all.

Moreover, it must be remembered that the royal supremacy, or establishment, which is the same thing, makes the Church national; and this important truth was clearly seen by Henry VIII. when he used the expression, "the King's English Church and Congregation;"[1] the king's, that is, as the representative and head of the nation—the National Church, which it was not before. For the nationality of the Church does not consist, as some persons foolishly imagine, in every individual of the nation frequenting a church and making use of its services, but in the fact that every one may do so if he will. A parochial church is still the church of the parish, though half the parish may never enter its walls. The British Museum is a national institution, though two-thirds of the population never avail themselves of the opportunities it offers them. A bridge belongs to the nation, not because the whole nation passes over it, but because the nation has secured that right for all who are willing to use it. So things become national that were once the peculiar property of individuals, or of societies, by the nation taking them under its control; in other words, establishing them. A dissenting chapel holding two thousand worshippers is private property. It can shut its doors against whom it will. A parish church with only thirty in its congregation is national and cannot turn away a single parishioner. For by establishment the nation secures the services of the Church for every

[1] 31 Hen. VIII. c. 14.

individual in the nation, and in this case without any cost to itself. But before establishment, before the assertion of the royal supremacy, the Church was not national. It was a society governing itself, admitting to its privileges whom it would and excluding whom it would, from the highest to the lowest. It was utterly indifferent to the national will, as it was exempt from national control. *Now*, every Englishman, be he what he will, can obtain the ministrations of the National Church, and cannot be deprived of them except by the will of the nation, as expressed in its laws: *then*, he was dependent for this privilege on the will of the clergy; the Church was a distinct society in a society, ruling itself, making laws in relation to its own interests, occupied with the care of advancing its own influence and authority. Not without reason. For as the spiritual power appeared to be immeasurably superior to the temporal, it followed as a matter of course not only that the clergy should bear rule for the good of mankind, but that the laity should be excluded from all share of authority: or, in other words, as God had founded the Church, some other power than His had founded the nation. Nor is it easy to avoid the evil consequences which flow from such a notion when it has once taken possession of the minds of men.

So before the Reformation the Church was exclusive and independent, not national, existing for itself and not for the nation; a society apart from the nation. And though the theory of Hooker, that the Church and nation are coordinate, differing only as to the point of view from which they are regarded, may appear fanciful to some, there is no doubt that it expressed a conviction common in his own days. By the act of the Reformation the Church and the nation, formerly divided, had now become one society; in one sense the Church was the nation, in another sense, the nation was the Church. Nor would this, the truest and profoundest of all conceptions of our national life and being—full as it is of the wisest suggestions—have been so carelessly set aside, as visionary and antiquated, had men really understood the meaning of the word *National*. For Hooker did not imagine that Puritans, Roman Catholics, and Jesuits made use of the services of the Church of England in his days more than they do now; or that nationality meant the exact tale of so many heads at any given time. It is a modern notion to suppose that nationality depends upon numbers only, and as the majority varies nationality appears or disappears!

Establishment, then, is necessary if the Church is to be National, in the strict sense of the term; and of that Dissenters are perfectly aware, though they are not wise in wishing to get rid of establishment, utterly mistaking its real effects. For what possible disadvantage can it be to them, if the State secures for all members of the nation, Dissenters as well as Churchmen, their right to the National Church, if they choose to avail themselves of it? Suppose they do not, is it any injustice to them that the opportunity should be offered them? Would not the opposite be much more intolerable and oppressive? Would it not be far worse if all men had their part in the National Church except Dissenters? If every man in the nation, whatever his worth or condition, might attend the services of the Church, and enter its gates at his pleasure, except a Dissenter, would not this appear a most harsh and unjustifiable exclusion? Suppose that his dissent is a mere matter of preference, involving in his own mind no conscious hostility to the Church—does he think it would better accord with his feelings of justice and equality if he and his children were excluded from the Church, whatever the case might be, or admitted only on sufferance, whilst the nation had claimed it for all others as a right? I cannot imagine any distinction more galling or more offensive. Yet this is what the Dissenter is aiming at in his desire to get rid of establishment. For it is establishment, and establishment alone, that secures for him this right in common with the rest of his fellow-citizens.

But suppose that he is content to forego it; to be wholly excluded from his part in the Church; it can surely be no injustice to him if others desire to avail themselves of the opportunity thus offered and secured to them by the nation. So long as he himself is not compelled to go to church, what wrong can it be to him if others go? Nay, is it not a great injustice that because he despises his privilege he should wish and endeavour to deprive others of theirs? For as establishment secures that right, disestablishment annuls it. If Churchmen are desirous to have it, if they think that establishment contributes to the good government of the Church and their own welfare as Christians, why should the Dissenter object? Establishment does not affect him. It does not touch dissenting ministers, chapels, or congregations. It does not interfere with any of their rights or infringe their personal liberty. If it is sought, on the other hand, to weaken and impair the Church's influence, in the belief that it is detrimental to the good and peace of society, how is disestablishment to effect that object? For disestablishment is simply to place the Church back into the position and authority it held before it was established[1]; to make it wholly independent of the temporal power; to leave it to itself and its own self-government; to allow it to make canons and articles of faith, and insist on all men's compliance with its dictates as a condition of being admitted into its communion; to exclude the Dissenter from any share or participation in it; to erect a society second only in influence to the nation itself, and possibly stronger than the nation. Does this seem desirable? The clergy might perhaps think so—and it will be an evil day for the tranquillity of this nation when they come to think so. But can the Dissenter? He who already complains that the Church has an undue share of power, that it is not conciliatory, that it treats Dissenters with haughtiness and keeps them at a distance, will he by disestablishment leave the

[1] See p. 287, etc.

Church free and unfettered to provide for its own interest and advancement, exempted from all control?

Establishment, then, is necessary, not only to secure to the laity and even to Dissenters themselves their due rights and privileges, but also to maintain that moderation and regard for others which religious fervour and enthusiasm are apt at times to overlook. The Church of England is as moderate and tolerant as any Church or any religious society, I doubt not; but if it is not indebted to establishment for these virtues, establishment has been favourable to their development. It is not easy to say how much the national control to which the Church is thus subjected has in difficult and in trying times kept it free from excesses into which it might otherwise have fallen. For there are periods when Churchmen, as well as Dissenters, are apt to imagine that the interests of religion committed to their charge ought to exclude all other considerations. The tremendous importance of the truths they have to teach blinds them to the value of others not less momentous, but apparently, for the time, less imperative. As we do not desire to see a return to that temper of mind which forced *The Solemn League and Covenant* on this nation and turned every clergyman out of his living under the false pretence of malignancy, so should we equally deplore to see a repetition of the Bartholomew Act. For that moderation, then, which the Church of this country has in general observed, for that just balance between the rights of the clergy and laity which has contributed so much to the good understanding and tranquillity of both, we are not a little indebted to establishment; and all would deplore the day, and not least Dissenters themselves, when the safeguards for this moderation were withdrawn by any delusive panacea of disestablishment.

But national establishment and a national Church involve the necessity of certain fixed laws and prescribed forms of faith. The Church and the nation must clearly understand each other. For how can the nation establish that of which it is ignorant? Or how can the Church conscientiously submit to a control, the extent of which is undefined? The nation must know what those religious rights and privileges are to which the Church admits its members, and what the conditions; or how can it assert those rights if they are violated? If all members of the nation have a right to be baptized on professing certain articles of faith, it is necessary that those articles should be fixed, it is necessary they should be known, it is necessary they should be uniform. If the nation attempts to change them it violates the rights and independence of the Church; if the Church attempts to alter and to modify them it invades the rights of the laity.[1] So it is with all the ministrations of the Church. The laity cannot insist upon partaking of its ministrations, or be admitted to its communion, unless they are willing to comply with the conditions agreed upon; the clergy cannot

[1] [Facts strongly confirm this view. Ever since the Reformation, legislation as to the Prayer Book, Articles, etc. has, with a few exceptions easily accounted for, been the joint work of Parliament and Convocation. While matters of *substance*, whether doctrine or ritual, have thus been dealt with by Church and State jointly, *discipline*, or the maintenance of the doctrine and ritual so settled, has been under the control of the State. Legislation dealing with discipline has been the work of Parliament without Convocation. I have discussed this distinction in detail in my book "Church Courts," chaps. i, ii, iii.

In contrasting, as he does throughout, the Church and the laity (see p. 228), Mr. Brewer is following the example of all the writers of the Reformation period. The Church for legislative purposes, and so far as power and authority were concerned, was identical with the clergy. The "spiritualty" in the Reformation Statutes means the clergy. See 24 Henry VIII, ch. 12. L.T.D.]

alter or interpret those conditions in conformity with their own notions. That which has been ordained for the general good cannot be transgressed, altered, diminished or augmented, at the dictate of individual whim or caprice. No innovation in any order can be allowed which rests on less authority or less general consent than that by which such order was established. Suppose the clergy wish to enact some canon or constitution which they deem beneficial to the Church, who is to make it authoritative? The nation? We know no other power. But suppose the nation does not consider such constitution beneficial either to the Church or itself. Can any obligation, any consideration of justice, bind a nation to impose upon itself and its posterity what it is convinced is injurious to both? Suppose the laity should insist on altering the creeds and depraving the sacraments, can they bind the consciences of the clergy? Is it not clear that both have their rights, and if any alteration is to be made both must agree in the alteration? If not, the Church ceases to be national. It is the Church only of one portion or of the other; of the clergy, if the clergy be supreme, of the laity, if the latter overrule.

Rightly, therefore, is it insisted that a national Church must aim at a certain amount of identity in its religious teaching. We believe that our Church is built upon the foundation of Apostles and Prophets, and that foundation does not change. We believe that our faith and the faith of our fathers was the faith of Apostles and Prophets. Nay, more, we should suspect a faith that had not this identity, that changed with the times and the seasons, that varied and winded with the caprices, the notions, the fashions, the science of men; for the faith which we believe was that which God taught, and not man, and therefore, like Himself, is invariable. It has, then, an identity, as the sun has an identity of light and the earth of motion.

But if it be an undue limitation on the Church's freedom, that it must not impose new articles of faith or vary the terms of its communion, I ask, What new creeds or *credenda* would the Church have imposed beyond those it insists upon already, supposing it had never been established? Judging from the example of other Churches, or of our own previous to establishment, there are certainly none that we should, as Protestants, have been willing to accept. Have not Dissenters been exempt from establishment? Have they not had free liberty to discover and impose upon themselves any new article of faith, if they could have discovered any? Would they not have made the most of it if they had, seeing that any clear, undoubted article of faith, warranted by Holy Scripture, held by themselves and ignored by the Church of England, would have given them greater weight and authority with the people of this land than the most fervid and fluent denunciations of establishment? Wisely, the Dissenters have made none, and the only Church that has made such a discovery has left us an example to be avoided. For of all liberty that can be allowed to a Church, or which any Church can claim, there is none so perilous as that of declaring new articles or definitions of faith. A nation may recede from a law which it has made; it may allow the law to fall into oblivion when the circumstances which justified its enactment have passed away, or its judgment has grown more clear and more mature; for laws are temporal, but articles of faith are eternal. "The Church hath authority," says Hooker, "to establish that for an order at one time which at another time it may abolish; and in both may do well. But that which in doctrine the Church doth now deliver rightly as a truth, no man will say that it may hereafter recall and as rightly avouch the contrary. Laws touching matter of order are changeable by the power of the Church; articles concerning doctrine, not so. We read often in the writings of Catholic and holy men touching matters of doctrine: 'This we believe; this we hold; this the prophets and evangelists have delivered; this martyrs have sealed with their blood and confessed in the midst of torments; to this we cleave as to the anchor of our souls; against this, though an angel from Heaven should preach unto us, we would not believe.'"[2] This being so, and the consequences so tremendous, it cannot be thought any intolerable hardship that the Church of England is not allowed to declare any new doctrine, or insist on any new articles of faith. If this be the limitation imposed upon it by establishment, that limitation is no less salutary than it is necessary.

With good reason, then, as the Church is national, it cannot for its own sake, or the sake of the nation, alter or modify its creeds, its canons, or its discipline, without the consent

[2] Eccl. Pol. ii. p. 33.

of the nation; for the nation and every one in the nation is concerned in that alteration. And this not only because if it makes or modifies any creed, constitution, or canon, it must necessarily affect the rights of its lay members and make laws for others without their concurrence; but because all laws so made, whilst the Church continues to be established, would not be its own laws merely, resting solely on its own authority, but also the laws of the nation, whose voice it uses, whose function and representative it is in all things spiritual—as much as the judges of the land are the permanent representatives and embodiment of the judicial faculties of the nation, or the House of Lords of its hereditary aristocracy, or the House of Commons of its immediate and passing thoughts, desires, and emotions.

But there is yet a more obvious and unanswerable reason why the Church cannot alter its standards, arising out of the nature of the Church's endowments. Of those endowments the Church has only the usufruct, not the absolute possession; for it neither can alienate nor exchange them, nor transfer them from one purpose to another. On what conditions those endowments were first given it is now idle to enquire, for the nation has long ago settled that question for itself, and determined by solemn Acts of Parliament its sense of that matter. In that decision all have acquiesced, as they do and must acquiesce in all Acts of Parliament so long as they remain in force. In that acquiescence both the laity, for whose religious instruction and comfort those funds were given in the first instance, and the clergy, who are to teach and be supported out of those funds, are included. Clearly, then, here are two rights: the right of the laity in every parish, thus endowed, to the instruction and ministration of the Church of England by its accredited ministers; and the right of those ministers to the enjoyment of the funds thus given, so long as they instruct the people committed to their charge and dispense the Word and Sacraments according to the faith and usages of the Church of England. The funds are in trust for the benefit of both; they belong absolutely and exclusively to neither. The conditions are fixed, and neither party, separately or conjointly, can infringe them, for both have in them no more than a temporary and conditional right. Consistently with good faith and honour, the minister cannot hold these funds and break the conditions on which he has received them, by neglecting, or contradicting, or impugning the creeds, confessions, sacraments, doctrines, and order of the Church of England, of which he is the representative. Nor can his congregation require that he should; nor can he justly comply with such requirement. If he transgresses and neglects the conditions, not merely his whole congregation and every individual in it, but every individual in his parish, has lawful cause of complaint, because his right is invaded. So long as the minister does his duty according to the faith and teaching of the Church of England contained in the Book of Common Prayer, so long he is secure. That is the rule from which neither can depart, and these are the conditions to which both must adhere. Suppose there is a dispute as to the conditions; shall the clergyman decide? Shall he be permitted to teach as he pleases? Shall he admit to his ministrations or exclude from them, at his own option, those for whose religious instruction and consolation these funds were provided? That is clearly impossible. Shall, then, his congregation decide the conditions on which he shall minister? That would be a violation, not only of the rights of the clergyman, but of the judgment of the whole nation, which has determined those conditions. There must be some appeal to a judge independent of both, and that is to the bishop in the first instance, to the sovereign, as the head of the Church and supreme over all persons, ecclesiastical as well as civil, in the last resort; and this is the result of establishment. For without that supremacy, in any dispute between the clergy and the laity, it would not be possible for justice to be done. One or other party would then be the judge of his own right. The decision must rest either with the clergy or his congregation. If with the clergy, we have the sacerdotal autocracy of the Church of Rome; if with the congregation, the arbitrary democracy of dissent—the disciple is set above his master.

So long, then, as establishment remains, the rights of both parties are maintained by an impartial tribunal, and a fixed rule of faith and doctrine laid down in the Book of Common Prayer; a rule from which neither can depart, and into which no innovations can be introduced without the consent of the whole nation, both spiritual and temporal. For, consistently with its repeated declarations that the Book of Common Prayer is agreeable to the Word of

God and the teaching of the Gospel, the nation cannot now break faith with the Church and insist, without its concurrence, on essential alterations. Nor can the clergy, on the other hand, be permitted, without consent of the nation, to make changes in the Prayer Book, which is, in fact, the Magna Charta of the religious liberties and rights of all. And as establishment has thus secured for us a supreme and impartial tribunal, in whose decisions both clergy and laity have generally acquiesced—a blessing peculiar to this nation—so has it brought with it, as a necessary consequence of establishment, a Book of Common Prayer, common both to clergy and to laity—a blessing also of the highest importance, and peculiar also to the Church of England. There is no *common* prayer either among Roman Catholics or Dissenters; but with the former, prayer is essentially the service of the priest, and among the latter, it is the prayer of the minister. It is purely sacerdotal or ministerial—vicarious, that is, in both instances,—and independent of the congregation. For as there can be no common prayer without a fixed form of prayer, so can there be no common prayer without establishment. It is of the very essence of voluntary churches to admit no authority external to their own, and to be bound, as Dissenters boast, to no unchangeable form of prayer or doctrine.

Thus by its establishment we have secured to the Church and the nation, not only a due observance of their respective rights, but a permanent standard of pure faith and a common expression of that faith, as pure, noble, majestic, and catholic, as it is inimitable. Different bodies of Dissenters prefer different forms of ministration. They will insist on extempore prayers and preaching; yet few of them venture to depart very widely from the faith and practice of the Church of England, or, if they do, they lose all chance of permanent popularity. For those religious societies are precisely the most influential that differ least from the National Church; a conclusive evidence that there is a native strength in the established Church beyond what appears to careless observers, as expressing more completely than any other body our profoundest national convictions. Thus by its establishment, the Church tends to establish in the minds even of those who dissent from it a form of religious belief and practice not altogether dissimilar from its own. It is the fullest standard of our national belief; and the Church is national in this sense, that if it does not include the whole nation amongst its worshippers, it embodies more thoroughly than any other society the religion accepted by the people at large.

CHAPTER IV.

OBJECTIONS TO ESTABLISHMENT CONSIDERED AND
ANSWERED.

It appears, then, that establishment is not so much for the benefit of the Church, as of the laity. The Church receives no advantage, no accession of wealth, power, or pre-eminence from being established by the State, but the reverse. By establishment the State controls the action of the Church, secures for the nation the services of a great religious society, which, as a nation, it has done nothing to found, nothing to encourage, nothing to advance. By establishment it gratuitously secures the active co-operation of a large body of men, devoted to the most vital and most important of all duties—the training of the members of the State in religion and virtue as Christians, in loyalty and obedience as citizens. For this co-operation it has never, as a nation, paid anything, and it never does pay. By establishment, also, it exercises a control over the funds and endowments of the Church, funds and endowments given by the piety and munificence of its individual members, to which the nation, as such, has contributed nothing. The services, the energies, the means and resources which are left at the disposal of all other societies, religious or otherwise, for the exclusive promotion of their own individual interests, are on the part of the Church, and of the Church alone, claimed by the nation for its own purposes. The individual interest and advancement of the Church are a secondary consideration, never allowed for a moment to come into competition with the primary purpose of establishment. For no one doubts that, while the State would rigidly and strictly interfere with any action of the Church, which might affect the rights it has claimed for the laity and their interests, it always has been supremely indifferent to the interests of the Church itself, so far as any active aid, support, or pecuniary assistance was concerned. Denunciations of the Church may be heard on all sides in the House of Commons—bitter reproofs of real or supposed transgressions or neglect of its duties—trenchant exposures of its weakness and shortcomings; but aid, encouragement, and support, never. No Chancellor of the Exchequer includes a single item in his budget for the expenses of the National Church, and no House of Commons would allow it if he did. Presbyterianism has had its *Regium Donum;* Maynooth its annual grant. Science, geography, maritime adventure and experiment, any pressing temporal necessity, find a flexible and exorable Chancellor of the Exchequer. But the Church, never. The expansion of commerce and manufacture, daily increasing the wealth of the nation and altering the proportions of our population until their religious instruction becomes unmanageable, outstrips the resources and machinery of the Church. But the nation, as such, has never touched the burthen so much as with its little finger. It has left the Church alone and unaided to struggle with the rising flood of immorality, atheism, and discontent. Yet but for those efforts government would have been paralyzed, and commerce engulfed in revolution. Establishment, then, is wholly a benefit on one side, and that on the side of the nation, not of the Church.

But establishment, as I have said, of necessity involves fixed forms and confessions of faith. And as these things are thought to be wholly incompatible "with freedom of conscience," absurd and mischievous when made the "standard of every man's religious convictions," incompatible with the advance of spiritual knowledge, which knows no limits, "dead dogma" as compared with the living realities of religion—(let me not be held responsible for this fashionable jargon)—men are beginning to consider whether we do not pay too dear for establishment, and whether in the plenitude of their enlightenment and the idleness of their dreams it would not be better that the State should have no established religion.

Let men face, which philosophers seldom do now-a-days, the practical results of their new-born theory. Of course, if disestablishment be all that is aimed at—in other words, the abrogation of the royal supremacy, and the control which the nation thereby exercises over the Church—the Church, if it merely regarded its own interests, could feel no objection. If the State is willing to part with that authority, patronage, and interference it has hitherto claimed in the affairs of the Church, why should the Church be dissatisfied? If it is to appoint its own bishops and deans, to summon its convocations, to enforce its own constitutions and canons, to have unrestricted freedom in reforming or modifying its creeds, confessions, and ritual, to exclude from its services whomsoever it pleases, to baptize or to bury at its own option—that, truly, is no very great sacrifice for the Church to make; and that is disestablishment. I am only afraid that the proposal is far too tempting, and that the Church would be only too willing to accept it, even should it be clogged with the condition of removing the bishops from the House of Lords, though they do not sit there, as some people imagine, by virtue of establishment.

But will the laity consent? for it is they that will have to make the real sacrifice by disestablishing the Church, and not the Church itself. Will they be content to leave the whole power of the Church in the hands of the Church, or, which is much the same thing, in the hands of the clergy?[1] Will they make the clergy paramount in all spiritual matters, and themselves and their children dependent for instruction and spiritual guidance on the grace of the clergy? They may perhaps do so, but they have not yet shown much inclination that way. Nay, more, when one considers the strong feeling of resentment which they entertain even now when any single clergyman attempts to act entirely independently of his congregation, and the general impression that the laity ought to be admitted to greater influence in the deliberations of the Church, it is not very probable that they will part with that systematic control exercised by them far more efficiently, by means of establishment, than they could exercise for themselves. They would find their admission to diocesan synods and parochial councils a poor compensation for the loss of that effective recognition of their rights which is secured to them by the present arrangement. No layman, I am convinced, however loyal to the Church, will be found in the ranks of disestablishers when he begins to understand what establish-

[1] [See p. 211, note.]

ment really means; for no one, I think, considering the services and necessities of the Church, will propose to diminish its endowments, still less to transfer them to Dissenters. That being so, disestablishment, pure and simple, is nothing more than the complete independence of the clergy of all control on the part of the laity—a result not very likely to meet with the acceptance of laymen.

As then establishment is little else than a necessary condition of the Church arising from its influence, wealth, and importance, it is as well to consider how far it is amenable to the charges brought against it by the friends and enemies of the Church of England. Is it true that establishment imposes restraints upon the freedom of conscience? Does it discourage and discredit inquiry, deaden the conscience, and place the clergy under legal definitions and restrictions unfavourable to their spiritual and intellectual advancement? Dissenting ministers and Roman Catholic priests are wholly free from establishment. Are they more conscientious in their lives than the clergy of the Church of England? Does the world turn from the theology of the Church of England, from its Prayer Book and its divines, to drink at the freer and more living waters of the unestablished theology of dissent? Are Hooker, Jeremy Taylor, Barrow, South, and Butler, all born under the blighting effects of establishment, no more studied and regarded? Are the unestablished divines of the Baptists, Independents, and followers of Wesley, so much more esteemed, that the household worthies of the Church of England are forgotten in the superior development of "the spiritual and intellectual nature" of dissent? Dissent has been no more established by law than science has been. It has not been "petrified into an unchangeable standard and protected by statute against the smallest alteration." Yet where are its great discoveries, its wonderful advances in theological truth, its ardour, its independence, its freedom, all of which are said to be wanting to the established Church? It would be as cruel as it would be ridiculous to push this argument further. To expose these false pretences, their utter unsoundness and unreality, is superfluous.

But there is a class sprung up among ourselves that is never tired with ringing the changes upon "dead dogma" and a "living faith." Now there is no more necessity in the nature of things that dogma should be dead than that faith should be living. If we may judge by their effects, creeds, articles, and confessions (and if these are not dogma, what are?), are no less vital, operative, and energetic than faith itself. But the contrast insisted on is absurd, for there can be no religious faith without dogma. He who puts his trust in another, be it in another's love, or honesty, or protection, must form some distinct conception of the being in whom he believes. He must believe that such a being is good, pure, and trustworthy; that his nature is such that he may be relied on. These conceptions are dogmas— determinations, that is, of his own mind, whether expressed in words or not.[3] And

[3] This is the absurdity into which modern thinkers are apt to fall when they contrast righteousness with dogma, and speak of the former as being spontaneous or natural, and the latter as artificial or acquired; whereas the one is quite as natural as the other. For though in matters of opinion alone the mind is not absolutely constrained to form any determination, yet, when opinion is carried out into practice, some determination—that is, some dogma—must be formed; men must resolve whether this action or that be conformable to the rule of right, and what that right is. Such declamation against dogma is puerile—Philistinism in its vapidest form; for all society, all social manners, all legislation, all administration of the law itself, all natural prudence rest upon dogma—that is to say, on certain determinations accepted by the general consent of society. This ab-

whilst in our intercourse and association with others we do and must form some such conceptions of their nature as these, the only difference between individual dogma or determinations, and dogma as embodied in

surdity is connected with another when they are denounced—with no small contempt—who are said to accept, without proof, the elementary truths of religion, and it is affirmed that these truths "are not proven." Proven to whom? I ask; and to whose satisfaction? And proven how? Must every elementary truth in practice be proven to every man's satisfaction before it can be permitted to stand? Must the elementary truths of manners and morals, and ordinary prudence, be proved before they can be assumed and acted on? The notion is preposterous. Their proof is in the general assumption of them, and remains valid and conclusive until some one shall be able to step forward and show, beyond possibility of denial, that the general assumption is erroneous. It is a dogma of good manners that the man shall give place to the woman. Are we to be told that this dogma must not be assumed and acted on because "it is not proven"? Moreover, what is meant by "proven"? Proven how? By the arguments that satisfy the mathematician, the logician, or the experimental philosopher? In the prudence of active life the judgment does not wait for scientific arguments, but is governed by probability alone; and not only by the balance of probability; for if in the attainment of any good there is any probability whatever, men act, and are bound to act, by that probability alone. If there was any probability that by passing through such and such a field a man would find £50, he would feel he was bound to act upon that single probability alone, and to assume it as a sufficient and conclusive reason for so doing, though the probability of *his* finding the £50 were as a hundred to one against him. Will any one venture to assert that there is *no probability whatever* in the personality creeds and articles of faith, is that the former is the determination of the individual judgment, and the latter of the Church, the careful harvest of many minds and many ages. The New Testament sets before us the life of One Who called God His Father and Himself the Son of God. How can any man believe in Him who either rejects these words—the highest insult to His majesty—or, accepting them, puts no meaning upon them, which is scarcely less an insult? He must then determine in his own mind in what sense Christ called Himself "the Son of God;" in other words, a dogma. If he resolves for himself, or accepts it from another, that Christ is the Son of God and is God, directly he has expressed this conviction in words it becomes a dogma; in ordinary sense, a deter-

of God or the primary elements of Christianity? If there is any—the very least—for religious prudence they are as much proven as if they could be mathematically proved, and we are as much bound to act upon them as if they were scientifically demonstrated. But if any one asserts that there is not the least probability of their truth, why should I accept *his* dogma before the dogma of those whom he censures, for they at least have the sanction of time and experience, which his dogma has not? So, in denouncing dogma, our modern theorists are the most dogmatic of all authors. But as they have never carefully considered what dogma is, they have never attempted to comprehend what it is in relation to a religious society such as the Church, or in its relation to the individual members of which every Church is composed.

mination as to the nature of Christ derived from Christ's own words. He does so equally if he rejects the meaning put upon them by his fellow-Christians. The Unitarian and Dissenter are not more free in this respect than the member of the Church of England. They are as much bound by their negative as the Church of England by its positive dogma. He is as much a dogmatist who affirms that Christ is not God as he who asserts He is God; who asserts that baptism is not necessary to salvation as he who affirms the contrary. And as in all matters relating to practice men must form certain opinions, for they cannot act without them, there can be no practical, active piety without this determination of the mind; that is, without dogma.

The question, then, is not the opposition of faith to dogma; nor whether we shall reject dogma altogether; but whether these determinations in theology are unnecessarily multiplied by the Church of England, and whether it should insist on them or not. Not to insist upon them at all would not be to get rid of dogma, as some imagine, but to allow every man to form his own and obtrude them on others if he could. It would leave every man, woman, and child, however ignorant, incompetent, and liable to error they might be, to form opinions at hap-hazard upon the most vital and most momentous of all questions—and that where error leads to fatal results, and, once entertained, corrupts the judgment and disqualifies it from discovering the truth. Suppose the Church sees this, and the infinite danger arising from it, and, touched with compassion and prompted by a sense of its responsibilities, stretches out a helping-hand. Suppose it says, "This is the way, walk ye in it." This is the way which long experience and the wisdom of the wise, in all ages, has found to be the right way. May it say this, or may it not? If it may not, what becomes of its functions as a Church, as a guide of the blind, as the preacher of truth and righteousness? Its function as a Church ceases altogether. If it may, then in this case it must; for "to him who knoweth to do good and doeth it not, to him it is sin." If, then, it is bound to give such directions, and, giving them, to insist upon them—which follows as a necessary consequence—it may and must insist upon dogma; for dogma is nothing more than the determination of the Church in matters of faith where men have gone wrong, or are liable to go wrong. In other words, it follows, from the very essence of a Church, that it must guide, direct, and teach; that is to say, it must insist on creeds and confessions. And, further, it is guilty of dereliction of its duty if it does not. The more or the less must be determined by circumstances, and cannot be measured by any fixed rule, à priori.

And the same must be said of that uniformity of faith and dogma of which some complain. For, in the first place, uniform laws and rules are in their nature better than those which are always shifting and varying. How shall men know what to teach, or how to educate, if the Church itself is uncertain? How shall they prepare themselves for the battle if the trumpet give an uncertain sound? Even supposing, then, that the rules laid down by the Church were not precisely adapted to all alike, that creeds and forms of belief might with some advantage be varied to suit different intellectual conditions, it does not follow that the advantage to be gained would outweigh all the disadvantages. And the same remark applies here as it does to the Book of Common Prayer. Notwithstanding the far greater difficulty of finding any uniform expression for the religious sentiments of mankind, no one now imagines that we should be gainers by abolishing the Prayer Book and attempting to find one more elastic, or by bringing out a new one from year to year, or by having many instead of one.

And further, if notwithstanding the varieties of human minds and their intellectual inequalities, there is beneath them all a broad basis of a common and uniform nature; if the temptations and dangers of men, though not exactly, are pretty much the same; if the main errors into which they are liable to fall, or against which it is most needful to guard them, be tolerably constant, there is great reason why creeds and confessions, intended for large masses of men, should be constant and uniform also. The exact determination of this question must be left with the Church; for the most obvious of all reasons, as I will show presently.

It has often been said that no man has a right to impose his own faith upon another, or interfere between a man's conscience and his God; which may be true, but is wholly irrelevant. For what man does or can impose his own faith upon another? Who can compel another to be a member of the Church of

England, or a Roman Catholic, or even a Nonconformist, against his will? We are not living under the Inquisition. We have no penal laws even to fine a man if he refuses to go to church.

It may be wise in the State to remove religious disabilities and cease to insist on an explicit uniformity of faith; but then, that is because it has not been found expedient to do so. The State may well shrink from the task which theologians have found impossible. It may decline attempting to effect that by force which they have failed to effect by reason. But if the advocate of disestablishment tells us that the State must not interfere in matters of religion, because religion is an affair between a man and his God, he must either assume that the State must not interfere in anything, or in his philosophy there is no God and no conscience in any other matters than those that are purely religious!

But there are some who object to establishment and the fixed forms of faith connected with it, on other grounds. To these I must refer, even at the risk of seeming to depart from the immediate purpose of this chapter, as their opinions, though of very little validity in themselves, have made a deeper impression upon the staggering and confused imagination of this age than, considering their essential feebleness, we ought to have expected. To those who object to establishment and fixed forms of belief, not because they care for one or the other, but because in getting rid of the forms they imagine they will get rid of the truths contained in them, I have nothing to say. It is not to creeds, or confessions, or articles, they object, but to Christianity itself; and if they thought that creeds were destructive of the Christian faith, they would be as great advocates for creeds as they are now forward in denouncing them. They hope to quench the light of the sun, and foolishly imagine they can do it. They would rather return to the glimmering lights of heathenism than live under the full light of the Gospel; and their disbelief and discontent are more the result of demoralized imaginations and of weak brains, than of any strong and settled convictions, or of any real love of the truth itself.

But there are others who object to forms of faith upon higher motives, as they think. They imagine that forms are only transient; that faith follows the same law as physical development, and therefore as the forms in which it is enshrined become too narrow for its energies, so far from being preservative they are destructive of it. Further, they think in proportion as men value forms they must neglect the life and reality concealed beneath them. Their opposition, then, to permanent expressions of faith and doctrine takes not the shape of hostility to Christianity, except so far as they have persuaded themselves that Christianity itself is a form doomed, like other forms, to pass away, but it is owing to an excessive regard for the truth itself.

Now I will not insist on the absurdity of applying to one set of facts the same mode of reasoning which is adapted to another set of a totally different nature;—that is, the material facts, of which sense is the only ultimate tribunal, and the facts of our spiritual nature, of which faith is the supreme judge, and not sense. This is as unscientific as it would be to assume that all proof must be of one nature only. With equal justice might the mathematician demand of the experimentalist the rigid demonstration of abstract science, or the politician or the man of business decline to act or accept any plan of operation, or any conclusion, which did not satisfy the rigid demands of the logician. The facts of various departments of knowledge challenge their own methods of demonstration, and what is applicable to one is totally inapt when applied to another. Moreover, the facts of experimental philosophy are innumerable; if not absolutely, yet relatively to us; for the book of nature is not wholly unrolled to us, and natural science every day enlarges its borders. It is subject to continual modifications and changes as Nature gives up her secrets and fresh facts and observations are imported from regions never explored before.

But with the Christian faith it is wholly otherwise. The facts concerning its nature, origin, and meaning lie within a very small compass. They are contained exclusively in the Bible. This Church or that, this teacher or the other, may combine them in different ways and draw different conclusions from them. But the facts themselves remain the same: they cannot be increased or modified by subsequent discoveries. As they were delivered by the Son of God, so they remain. Be it, as some have contended, that these evangelical facts have taken

R

a certain colour from the minds or circumstances of those who delivered them. What then? We must still accept them in the shape they have come down to us; for if we reject them in consequence of their shape, we can frame no judgment about them at all. This man or that may imagine that he can separate the outer form from the inner and more intrinsic; nor will any Christian deny that whilst "the letter killeth, the Spirit giveth life;" or that things spiritual "must be spiritually discerned;" but still, to the day of doom, when all is said and done, the facts of the Gospel will remain the same as they have come down to us, and no "delicate philology," no moral consciousness, or critical manipulation, will add to them one iota, or detract one iota from them. As they are not the facts, then, of experimental philosophy, nor the deductions of abstract science, but special facts made known to us in a special way, appealing to special faculties within us, with what consistency can the experimentalist or the mathematician insist upon wresting them from their proper order, character, and purpose, and treating them according to his own approved method? This is to transgress the elementary and primary caution of the philosopher, who condemns it as childish and puerile for men to be satisfied with one method of demonstration only—as puerile, to use his illustration, as to demand of the orator and the politician the rigid proofs of the mathematician, or of the mathematician the probable arguments of the statesman. The truths and facts of the Christian faith are to be judged by themselves, and in accordance with their own method; and whereas in history, authority, or the *Nubes Testium* (the Cloud of Witnesses), is the main tribunal, in logic and mathematics the pure reason, in physics the harmony of the phenomena, none of these, in matters of faith, have so great a cogency as the *via experimentalis* and personal conviction. It is by the latter, and not by the former, that Christianity, which is essentially practical, is to be judged; by the roughness, that is, the illogicalness, the contradictions of practice, which have a profound order beneath them; and not by the smooth, systematic precision of more scientific processes.

But further, as we must accept the facts of the Gospel in the form in which we find them, it is absurd to reject them on the grounds that Christianity itself is in a state of development, and a purer Gospel may possibly be in store for us. It is as absurd as if, accepting

Mr. Darwin's theory of development, we should refuse to consider what we are, or to act as we are, because in some indefinite ages ago we were less perfectly developed than we are now, and may be more perfectly developed in some millions of years to come. We must still walk, or ride in an omnibus, even should nature hereafter intend to complement us with wings, or even though, ages ago, we may have been incompetent of locomotion. We must still provide for our own wants and those of others, govern our children and ourselves, live according to the light which God has given us of Himself and our own nature, be temperate, chaste, loyal, and obedient, as if all mankind had always been precisely what they are now in the nineteenth century and development were an absolute fiction. Nay, Mr. Darwin himself would no more have thought of letting off a pickpocket, or a tradesman who had defrauded him, because mankind, in some future stage of existence, may be developed into a higher moral condition, than if he no more believed in his own theory than many others do. For all the ordinary duties and obligations of life development leaves us exactly as it found us; and, whether it be true or false, it does not alter a single moral or religious obligation. How can it?

For Christians themselves believe in a much more startling development than any which finds a place in Mr. Darwin's philosophy. They believe that they have a new life and new faculties, that they are transplanted into a new kingdom, brought into the presence of God Himself, sanctified by His Holy Spirit. They believe that these are realities—absolute changes in their condition from what they would have been had they not been Christians; more intense realities than any analogies of this life can represent—more than if, being African slaves, they had changed their skin and their condition; or, living in some dark and dismal cave, they had been brought into the presence of some great sovereign, such as the ruler of this country; or had been taken from the grave into the region of life and light. But this real and certain change in their condition—this new heaven to them and a new earth—does not in any way nullify or dispense with their duties as inhabitants of this world. They are as much bound to its duties and obligations as if they had never been Christians. They must be loyal, virtuous, friendly, good citizens, zealous in their callings, as if they had never heard of Christianity or partaken of its privileges. How, then, can it be supposed that any development of their material forms can dispense with their moral and religious obligations, or alter in the least any one single relation in which they stand to God or man? For the sanctions of piety, morality, and religion are immutable, and do not depend upon the outward forms of human nature. They are equally obligatory on the cultivated man and the savage, in the proportion that each can understand them; on the undeveloped intellect of the child as on the fully-developed intellect of the philosopher. And if we could suppose any class of mankind of higher or less developed faculties than our own, of men that could fly, or of men who had one eye instead of two, the case would remain the same.

For as it would be incredibly absurd in a farmer to refuse to cultivate his land, or sow his seed, because at some future period in the world's history both land and seed might be more highly developed than they are now, and be better adapted to the production of food; so would it be equally absurd, because at a previous stage of our existence the knowledge of farming was less perfect than now, land less carefully tilled, and corn either dwarfed or none at all, to go back to this state of things, to use a wooden hoe instead of a plough, to sow nothing but oats where wheat now grows, and rest contented with being as ignorant, unskilled, and clumsy as men were in a more imperfect stage of the world. For however his superior knowledge and skill have come to man, whether by the laws of development or otherwise, he is as strictly bound by all the laws of prudence, morality, and religion, to use his knowledge for the best, as if development had no share in it. Nor can he be excused if he refuses to do so; "for to him who knoweth to do good" (however that knowledge has come to him) "and doeth it not, to him it is sin." Whatever has been the condition of men, whatever it shall be hereafter, we must accept things as they are, and not imagine we can dispense with the duties and obligations which our *present* condition imposes upon us.

But there are many who will acquiesce in this argument and readily allow that we must receive Christianity in the form it has come down to us, with all its obligations. They will admit that the fulfilment of those duties, as they are known to us, is the necessary preparation for those that are to follow. As in the successive stages of our natural development from childhood to old age, each age has its tasks and its duties; as the child cannot neglect with impunity the tasks and duties of the child, because it is destined to grow up to manhood, so cannot the full-grown man dispense with his because he expects the development of old age. But they will urge that though Christianity is incumbent upon them in the form in which it now is, and not according to some possible form hereafter, of which no correct conception can be framed, and none can give any definite account, it does not follow that the Church has a right to impose upon them or others its own conceptions of those forms. For though it may be incumbent upon all believers to accept and insist upon Baptism, as enjoined by our Lord, it does not follow that we are bound to accept the conception and form of Baptism insisted on by the Church of England; and though there may be sufficient traces in Scripture of the existence of bishops, as a form of Church government, it does not follow that the form of episcopacy, as practised by the Church of England, is of necessity the right one, or is exclusively binding upon all that receive the Gospel. Or again, though it may be true that every article in the creeds may be found dispersed throughout the pages of Scripture, it does not follow that in the form in which they are collected and isolated from their context the Church has a right to impose them upon others. All this is no less true than it is apparent, and that for the most sufficient of all reasons—that as no man can be compelled to accept the creeds and discipline of the Church of England, without his own consent, the Church can have no right to impose them; at least if it has, it never attempts to use it. And that is true of all creeds and all religions. For no man is compelled to be a Baptist, or Unitarian, or Independent, or even a member of the Church of England against his will; and if he finds himself in that condition he can remove from it whenever he will. If I, for the better regulation of my household, adopt certain forms of religious instruction and domestic devotion, it would be absurd in me to insist upon forcing the same regulations on my neighbour, but if my neighbour desires to become my guest, still more if he wishes, with my consent, to take up his abode with me, it would be preposterous in him to insist that I must dispense with my regulations, because he does not like them, and complain that I was guilty of tyranny, and imposed them upon him, because I refused to comply with his dictation. And that is exactly the position of the Church of England. It imposes its creeds, its confessions, its articles upon no one except on those who wish to join its communion. It compels no one to remain in its communion if, after having joined it, he is not satisfied with its interpretation of Scripture, or with the regulations it deems indispensable for the government of its household. The Church is a society, and therefore must possess the inherent right of all societies, of judging what is right and doing what is best for its members. Nay more, as a society, and constituted as the Church is, it is bound to do this by the most solemn of all obligations, and cannot dispense with this necessity even if it would. That "unity of profession," those "prescribed articles of faith," of which complaint is sometimes made are a necessity inherent in its condition as a society; and unconditional freedom and independence exist no more among Dissenters than in the Church of England. For does any one imagine that a Baptist minister has such entire freedom that he may insist on the necessity of infant baptism, or an Independent condemn unepiscopal ordination, or a Unitarian defend the doctrine of the Trinity? Or may any of them insist on Transubstantiation, or even adopt the conclusions of Strauss? The very fact of a society implies that the will of that society, as a body, must overrule the individual will of each of its members. How, then, can there be unconditional individual freedom in any society? Dissenters have their creeds, their articles of faith, their dogmas, their discipline, no less than the Church of England; and therefore it is absurd to argue as if the one were entirely dependent and the others entirely free; as if establishment insisted on a "unity of clerical profession" and dissenting ministers might be as disunited and independent as individual conviction, caprice, or opinion led them. May any Baptist or Independent minister be a Unitarian and retain his ministry among the Baptists and Independents? May any Unitarian minister uphold the doctrine of the Divine Incarnation and retain his ministry among Unitarians? Unity, then, of clerical profession is not confined to establishment, nor is it the product of establishment.

But if it be said that there is more freedom for the dissenting minister than for the clergy of the Church of England, that is another question. It is true that neither dissenting ministers nor their congregations are bound to written articles of faith, to fixed creeds, or fixed forms of prayer, as the established Church is bound, for reasons already stated. But whether that is a real liberty or not may be questioned. By the creeds and formularies of the Church of England the liberties of all, whether clergy or laity, bishops or temporal rulers, are expressly and clearly defined. The bishop is as much bound by the Book of Common Prayer as his clergy, the clergy as the laity, and none can invade or trample on the rights of another, or substitute his own opinion or the passing opinions of his age, for the measured, thoughtful, deliberate expression of the Church as found in the Prayer Book. It is as great a security against rashness and arbitrariness on one side as against shallowness and impetuosity on the other. Within the limits allowed them all may walk freely and with the fullest security for their freedom. It is not so with Dissenters. True, they have no written creeds or formularies; but as much as the liberty dependent upon written laws is superior to that which has no such guarantee, so far is the liberty of the clergyman and his congregation superior to that of the Dissenter. For let no one suppose that Dissenters are so magnanimous that they will allow their minister to preach what he pleases, or propagate opinions which they consider to be dangerous, erroneous, or even unpalatable. But whereas the clergyman has the written word of the Prayer Book for his security and must be judged by that and by that only, the dissenting minister has no such advantage. He is amenable to the unwritten judgment of his congregation, guided by no fixed rules, liable to all sorts of influences, if competent not always impartial, if impartial not always competent. If, on the other hand, he is eloquent, influential, and indispensable to his congregation, he may trample on their rights with impunity. Plausible therefore as may be the representation of the freedom of dissent, it is more specious than real.

But further, it must be remembered that the advantage, in this respect, is entirely on the side of the Church of England. For though the established Church demands from those who join its communion adhesion to certain articles of faith, and insists, and rightly so, that its ministers, who are its accredited representatives and speak in its name, shall not contravene the letter or spirit of those articles, as expressed or assumed in the Prayer Book, those few and necessary articles excepted, clergy and laity alike have free range in the regions of theological research and speculation. Outside these limits none can be condemned, or deprived of their rights, even if they choose to entertain opinions at variance with those which are generally accepted. So long as a clergyman does not impugn those few primary articles of faith to which he has given his express assent, he is not liable to penalty, however absurd his opinions may seem to others. But that is not so and cannot be where such articles are not written and defined; and the dissenting minister may incur the displeasure of his congregation and their censure, not merely for contravening their notions in essential articles of faith, but in matters of religious opinion.

When, therefore, it is urged that establishment interferes with the freedom of the Church by insisting upon fixed forms of faith and dogmatic statements of doctrine from which no one is allowed to diverge; when, further, it is urged that such fixity of belief is unfavourable to the development of theological truth, we have to remember :—

First—That for every society whatever there must be some fixed rules and principles of association known to all its members, without which no society could exist; and that whenever any dispute arises as to those principles—their limitation, expansion, or their exact interpretation—the power must exist in the society itself of being its own interpreter and employing such precautions and safeguards for the explanation and preservation of its principles, as itself shall think fitting.

Secondly—But if this is and must be true of all societies, and is implied in their very nature, it is still more urgent in such a society as that of the Church itself, whose mission it is to teach and convert mankind and gather them into one great communion, not absolutely, but on certain conditions enforced and declared by its great Founder.

Thirdly—That a Church bound to teach the truth, but without the power to express what that truth is, or refusing so to do, or holding its peace when that truth is abused or disfigured, not merely by those outside its pale, but by those within it, is guilty not only of a gross anomaly, but of a flagrant neglect of its duty, and is false to its own functions. The way, however, in which it shall exercise its functions and exhibit its loyalty to its principles must be left to itself, to be exercised to the best of its conscience and ability.

Fourthly—That whereas, with the exception of those few fundamental articles of belief necessary to its communion, and their exact exposition when called in question, the fullest latitude is allowed to theological inquiry in all its branches, it is absurd to complain that the freedom of the Church is abridged. It is more absurd still to complain that it cannot add to these fundamental articles when, with all the supposed progress of theology, no fresh article of faith has yet been discovered essential to salvation and the acceptance of all men.

Fifthly—That in a Church so constituted as the Church of England, and possessed of endowments, to the use of which certain conditions are attached, it is indispensable to the freedom of all concerned that those conditions should be known and defined; and as those conditions in this case involve the necessity of agreement with the doctrines of the Church of England, it is necessary that those doctrines should be clear and explicit. For neither with justice to the laity, whose interests are concerned as well as its own, can the Church insist on imposing its own interpretation upon these articles of communion, or make new ones, without the consent of the laity, nor can the laity impose new articles on the clergy.

Therefore, the real question is not whether establishment abridges the liberty of the

Church, for no man on earth enjoys unconditional liberty, but whether, considering its position and the justice due to all parties, that liberty is abridged beyond what justice and expediency require; and whether we are warranted in believing, from the example of other unestablished religious bodies and our past experience, that more rapid progress would be made in theological truth without establishment than with it, and the rights of all be more completely secured.

CHAPTER V.

THE ADVANTAGES OF ESTABLISHMENT.

But, whilst establishment secures justice for all, it has in an especial manner secured for the laity a right and title in the Church they did not possess before. For though the Church be a society standing on distinct and independent grounds, by establishment that society has become as wide as the nation itself, as no other religious society is or can be. It is absurd to speak of it, as some do, as a *denomination*, like one of the sects. For the "Church of England" is the Church of England, as broad as England is, as wide and as lasting. It is so reputed and so taken in all the solemn acts and declarations of this nation, from its birth to the present moment; and the same cannot be said of any dissenting denomination whatever. And because it is the Church of England, all Englishmen, whether they like it or not, feel that they are connected with it; not bound indeed to use its services or render it obedience, but that somehow they are intimately concerned in what it does; a feeling in which they do not participate in regard to other religious bodies. For if any society of Dissenters, in the dissidence of dissent, were to split up into a variety of jarring factions, to assert or deny the Real Presence, to claim the most extravagant sacerdotal authority, the nation would listen, if it listened at all, to such proceedings with the utmost indifference and unconcern. Not a voice in the House of Commons would be raised in denunciation of such claims, nor an ear be open to hear it. But if the Church of England assumed a power, to which the laity conceived it had no just pretensions; if it preached doctrines at variance with the Prayer Book; if it openly repudiated the principles of the Reformation—the whole nation would be stirred and rocked from one end to the other.

This abiding, pervading, national interest in the Church of England, as such, conspicuous in every page of our history and in every great epoch of our national life, though never entirely absent at any time, became more direct and general by the establishment of the Church at the Reformation. Before that event the Church had grown up a self-governed and independent religious society. It ran its own unimpeded course, with little interference from the nation; except when its influence and authority appeared to overshadow the dignity and power of the Crown. Even the limitations imposed upon it were occasional and irregular; evaded and set aside, as the temper or circumstances of the Church or the nation offered the opportunity. There were, in fact, two societies, one secular, the other religious, if not always antagonistic, yet in some sense always opposed. It was the interest of the Church to maintain that opposition, to draw the line of demarcation between itself and the State as distinctly and broadly as possible. Religion for religious men, secular things for secular men; and as the judgment in temporal things must be left to the men of the world, all judgment and decision in spiritual things must be the exclusive concern of spiritual men. Could any definition be more precise, any course of reasoning more conclusive? The thought is still present in the minds of more than half of the world now—it is vigorous even among ourselves, and takes different shapes where least suspected. Men still think that the clergy ought to be restricted to clerical occupations, and that governments should have nothing to do with religion.

Nor was it possible, with so broad and impassable a barrier between the Church and the laity, with so rooted a conviction that religion was the exclusive concern of the former and this world of the latter, that consequences should not arise disastrous to both. Men cannot live without a religion; least of all can Englishmen; and if it be not a true one it will be a false one; and if not of the Gospel it will be the religion of fanaticism or superstition. For Deism has its fanaticism and superstition as well as its idolatry; its false lights and false gods. So good and evil divided the Church and the world between them, clergy and laity sinking deeper and deeper together. Moreover, as the laity disclaimed all right and interest in spiritual things, religion, left exclusively to the clergy, became of necessity more and more professional, less humane and less practical; found its chief places of resort in the schools and in cloisters; became daily more and more divorced from the bosoms and business of men; spoke to them in a language they could not understand, and lost its power as a living word.

In establishing the Church, in claiming their right and title to it, and therefore their undeniable right to protest against all forms of erroneous doctrine, our fathers at the Reformation were guided, consciously or otherwise, by a sound discretion, and consulted the truest interests of the Church itself. For however it may seem to some that the interposition in Church matters conceded to the laity at the Reformation was like mixing water with the wine, however that interposition may appear at times to interfere with the legitimate authority of the clergy, yet, as compared with the evils arising when the laity are superstitious or indifferent, who can doubt which state is the better? It is not merely that in the interest taken by the laity in the Church—an interest necessarily connected with this right and some share of power—we have a great security for the purity and moderation, for the zeal and activity of the Church of England—an interest salutary on the whole, though it may be sometimes officious—but the Church gains thereby a national strength and breadth of influence enjoyed by no other Church, where the laity have no such power. Unless the Church of England should alter greatly for the worse, unless it should become denationalized, it will never be with her as with the Churches of other lands. We shall never see the sanctuary left exclusively to the keeping of the clergy, nor the great body of the laity thundering at its gates with none but clerical champions to defend them. For no one can shut his eyes to the fact that the interest felt by the laity in the Church, admitted at the Reformation and developed since, has never wavered, never declined, but has grown with the growth and influence of the Church.[1] Was it so with the Churches of France and Italy? Were the statesmen and lawyers, the nobles and gentry of those lands, found among their Sunday-school teachers? Did they ever desire to be present at diocesan synods? Were their missionary meetings or Church-building societies crowded by devout and zealous laymen? Admit all that can be said of the munificent charities and exemplary devotion of many of the Roman Catholic clergy, yet in all that concerns the active co-operation of the laity, their interest in the Church, their sense of responsibility for its purity, its energy, its diffusion, no parallel can be found to our own.

Let, then, sentence be passed according to the facts, and it will be found that the benefits arising from establishment, and the consequent admission of the laity to a more active partici-

[1] The civil wars are only a seeming, not a real, exception to this statement.

pation of ecclesiastical privileges, far outweigh any occasional inconvenience. To have that right was to feel the responsibility connected with it—a responsibility, I admit, sometimes neglected, more often exercised in an ungracious manner; but a responsibility still of no mean advantage to the Church. For even when the laity cannot entirely recognize the excellence of its instruction, even when it does not appear wholly to meet their conceptions of certain religious truths—to be lukewarm when they are earnest, and dispassionate when they are decided—better such zeal than complete indifference. It is their Church, though they may dissent from its doctrines; theirs are its prayers and its ministrations, theirs also the communion of its saints and its forgiveness of sins. For what Dissenter does the Church turn from its doors? Against whom does it launch its anathema? Its very tenderness in this respect has been turned to its reproach. Unwilling to strike, it has done its best to win by patience and forbearance; and on its lips, as on those of its Divine Master, there are no reproofs. Were it not so, how many of those who have become faithful at the last would have been alienated by a sterner and severer policy!

Nor has this concession of a certain jurisdiction to the laity been without its advantages to the clergy themselves. The sense of their own right in the Church, the feeling that its welfare is intimately concerned with their own, has raised up friends and protectors in its behalf more than is generally suspected. Nor would this feeling fail to manifest itself if the Church were weaker, or if the attacks upon it were more successful. Englishmen do not care to come forward to help those who can help themselves. They are not sorry to see men and institutions put upon their mettle. And this is the grave mistake into which Dissenters and others are liable to fall; for seeing that these attacks upon the Church from various quarters fall fast and thick, and are regarded by the nation with apparent indifference, they are apt to think that the nation participates in their sentiments and shares their animosity. The truth is, that if the Church were in any real danger it would find troops of friends among the laity—silent and resolute men,—far more formidable as opponents than the forward and obtrusive. The Church only wants friends among the laity to find them. That help is to be had everywhere, among all classes, for the asking. For the Church of England *is* national, and that in a way its enemies little imagine. Bone of our bone, the outcome and impress of our national mind, either the nation or the Church must change greatly before we shall part with it. It requires no prophet to predict that the Church of England will never be disestablished unless it disestablishes itself.

In this respect I must contend that the establishment of the Church, and the consequent recognition of the right and title of the laity as represented by the Crown, was a great and beneficial act to all. It was as wise as it was beneficial; for it was so arranged that whilst it preserved these new rights for the laity, so important in their consequences, it secured their independence to the clergy. It steered between Scylla and Charybdis, avoiding the perils on which every other religious community has made shipwreck, neither depressing the spirituality under the laity nor the laity under the clergy. With very little exception, the Church and the State have worked harmoniously together; and the arrangement so beneficial to both has commanded the approbation of the greatest thinkers and divines amongst us. The slight oscillations of the machine have scarcely ever interfered with its effectual working; or ever been so violent as to create any latent or serious discontent. The great problem of the relation of the Church to the State—of all problems the most difficult with which a nation can have to grapple, and without the right adjustment of which national tranquillity is impossible—this problem, I say, our fathers, after many centuries and many sacrifices, solved at last, with such success that we have reaped the consequences in the harmonious co-operation of the two great essential factors of modern civilization, and of national progress. To this co-operation we mainly owe our greatness as a nation; to this we are indebted, under God, for the peace and stability we have so long enjoyed. From the same we derive that general moderation and forbearance which, without tempting us to sacrifice our independence or our principles, has kept us from the extremes of religious fanaticism on one side and of political convulsion on the other. The Church has always been on the side of order. Let those who look on this as a reproach consider what the results would have been if the Church, galled by undue subordination or fired by ambition, had always been on the side of disorder. It has insisted on loyalty to the

State as if the State had been its greatest benefactor, and not itself the greatest benefactor to the State, giving all and receiving nothing. And upon the whole the clergy have no reason to complain of their treatment by the laity. Without any subservience alternating with contempt—the lot of the clergy in other lands—the clergy among ourselves have been uniformly treated with an honest and manly respect due to their sacred functions. In every grade of English society they are received as friends and companions, as well as the messengers of a Divine Master; at least, where the minds of men are not blinded to all influences except those of rank and riches.

There is nothing more incomprehensible to a foreigner than the relations which exist in English society between the clergy and the laity, than the frankness and ease with which the clergy are admitted and received, and the footing of equality on which they stand with those who in social position and wealth are far above them. Is that no advantage to a country like this, absorbed and successful in the pursuit of wealth, and apt to exaggerate the means by which wealth is acquired? Is it no benefit to all that a class of men not more remarkable than others for genius or education, of moderate means and temperate tastes and habits, should be found in the society of the great and the wealthy, not merely as their confessors and religious advisers, still less as the ministers of their pleasures, but as associates, if not equals? Whilst such intercourse carries a generous sense of religion into the ordinary occupations, and even the amenities of life, it humanizes religion itself and checks its ascetic and professional tendencies. Religion becomes no longer the exclusive business of the priest or the formal task of Sundays and saints' days. We can see the clergyman, unlike the priesthood of other lands, co-operating with the layman in the religious and social improvement of the community without any impeachment of their mutual respect, without any fear that the sacred functions and character of the one, or the freedom and independence of the other, should be impaired by the contact. This harmonious interchange of sympathy and service smoothes away the asperity and angularity of distinct and in some respect of antagonistic callings. Out of the hostility and estrangement of alienated sentiment it creates kindlier feelings, too often buried beneath a load of coldness or indifference when the priest stands aloof in the seclusion of his sacred character, and the layman feels he has nothing in common with his guide beyond his hours in church.

As a nation, we are divided by fierce and irreconcilable party politics; probably we shall always be so. It is not desirable that we should add to those divisions, the fiercest and most irreconcilable of all, the bitter opposition of the Church and the State, or what is scarcely better, their mutual jealousy and distrust. For let no one imagine that the Church of this nation can ever be a weak and powerless body, established or disestablished. It can never be a feeble ally or a contemptible adversary.

Therefore the alliance, if alliance it can be called, between the Church and the State, no thoughtful politician, no lover of his country, would lightly tamper with. No man whose judgment is worth a straw would rashly disturb that settlement which cost our fathers so much thought and anxiety, and once undone could never be replaced. For of all the most wonderful and providential events of our history the establishment of the Church and its submission to the supremacy of the Crown, with so little bloodshed, is not the least wonderful. In the very zenith of its wealth and its power the Church bowed its neck and submitted to the yoke. It stooped to the supremacy of the nation, in the person of the sovereign, without a struggle; not in the face of an infuriated mob, not in the horrors of rebellion, when all laws and constitutional restraints are swept before the tempest, never to return or take root and rest again. It surrendered a portion of the independence it had been building up for years. Without noise, bloodshed and confusion, it passed into its new position, sacrificing the extreme justice of its claims without any rigid examination of the plea upon which that sacrifice was demanded. The position then assigned to it, it has held ever since without attempting to change it. It has recognized the will of the nation and acquiesced in it. The revenues of which it had been deprived it has carefully repaired by its own efforts and frugality, unaided by the State. Buffeted, afflicted, tempest-tossed, never, in its direst necessities or in the most rigorous demands on its exertions, assisted by the State, it has kept on its course irreproachably, though not without reproach. It has carried on the war against the infidelity and immorality of the land at times when infidelity and immorality, rising like a flood, bade fair to sweep away the ancient nations of Europe, and involve them all in irrecoverable ruin; at times, also, when wealth, luxury, and security, more deadly enemies to faith than even revolution, were waging impious warfare against all that was manly, noble, and divine. Unassisted and unrewarded, has it ever failed in its true mission of preaching the Gospel to the poor or urging their responsibilities on the rich? Have its churches been neglected, its congregations left to languish, its missionary efforts been intermitted? I speak of the general course and conduct of the National Church and clergy, as supposing that I am addressing readers who will not require those minute modifications and exceptions without which "uncandid dulness" fails to comprehend or accept any general statement.

But on estimating fairly and equitably the services rendered to the nation by the established Church from age to age, its general fidelity to its great mission, its freedom from turbulence and ambition, its moderation, its efforts in behalf of law and order, the "truth and soberness" of its teaching and ministrations, may we not ask—nay, it must and will be asked, for nations have their responsibilities as well as individuals—in what respect has the Church shown itself unworthy, that it should now be stripped of its endowments and distinctions? What has it done that it should be torn limb from limb and thrown into the seething cauldron of disestablishment, under the fallacious promise of renewed youth? If in previous ages it was less active, less conscientious, less alive to the duties of its sacred calling, is this the time for the State to repeal its privileges and confiscate its property, when, by the unanimous confession of friends and foes, it has put forth all its strength and everywhere displayed the utmost solicitude for the religious instruction of the people? That would seem to be not only the grossest injustice, but the greatest folly—the grossest injustice to whip and punish those who are doing the greatest service to the State in the best manner they can; the greatest folly to impair or destroy those services when they are most urgently required. If it could be shown that the clergy neglected their duty, that they were indolent, ignorant, and unable, that they were indifferent to the moral and religious evils of the day, it might have been assumed that these evils were traceable to establishment. The Legislature might have been called upon to annul a policy attended by such disastrous consequences. But it is admitted that the established Church has retained the purity of the faith in its creeds and articles; that its scholars and divines have

T

done heroic work, in defence of that faith, and the interpretation of those creeds; that it has brought up men whose genius and whose learning, though devoted to religion, have reflected an imperishable lustre on the nation itself. Nor can it fail to be admitted that the clergy, as a body, in their zeal, their efficiency, their parochial labours, have no superiors in this kingdom or out of it. If, then, all this be compatible with establishment, what reason have we for renouncing it? What more could we gain if the Church were disestablished?

It can hardly be necessary, after what has been said, to insist on the disadvantages of disestablishment. For if disestablishment be all that is intended, and not disendowment; in other words, if it is only proposed to emancipate the Church from the fetters of State control and that degradation which it is supposed to suffer in consequence of its connexion with the State, the only result of such a process would be to leave the Church in possession of the same influence and endowments it possesses at the present moment. Then all appointments in the Church would rest with the Church itself; then all acts of authority would emanate from itself; and the right of the laity to control its operations would cease, or extend no farther than the Church itself might think proper to permit. The assembling of its convocations, the modification of its creeds and articles of faith would be left wholly to its own discretion. Briefly, it would occupy precisely the same position as it occupied before the Reformation.[2] It might or it might not happen that its bishops would be excluded from the House of Lords, for that is a mere political arrangement and has nothing to do with establishment.

If the sovereign chose to call to that august assembly Cardinal Cullen or the President of the Wesleyan Conference, neither would the Roman Catholic Church nor Wesleyan Methodism be established by their admission. The bishops are the only members of that assembly who are peers for life, who have seats in that House not for their hereditary descent or their riches. They are, in fact, its only popular element; and whether their expulsion from the House might be of any advantage to them, to the House itself, or the nation in general, is for

---

[2] [See as to this *post*, p. 287. Mr. Brewer does not of course mean that what was abolished at the Reformation, e.g. the papal supremacy, would by disestablishment be revived. L.T.D.]

T 2

the nation to consider. As now, it would appear that nothing could be more reasonable or more sound than that they who have such extraordinary power, and are not likely to find their equals or superiors anywhere so much as in the House of Lords, should by this very contact with the laity learn what is passing in the minds of men, and be open to impressions they would not imbibe so easily if they only mixed with their clergy, and withdrew from all participation in secular matters. But this, as I have said, is simply a national question, and is wholly irrelevant to establishment.

But if under disestablishment more is implied, and disendowment as well as disestablishment be intended, then, undoubtedly, the problem becomes much more serious, and a vast number of practical considerations are involved of which we have a right to demand a much more satisfactory explanation than the advocates of disestablishment have yet ventured to give. We have a right to have it distinctly stated, supposing that the Church is to be deprived of its endowments, to what better purpose they propose to apply these endowments than they are applied at present. For nothing could be more absurd, dishonest, or impolitic, than for the State to take away its endowments from any body or society within its fold and apply them to worse purposes, simply on the ground that it possessed the power of so doing. We have a right to ask whether it is proposed to take away those endowments because they are misapplied or unnecessary. We have a right to ask whether the confiscation of local endowments, given for the spiritual instruction of the poorer classes and the maintenance among them of a permanent ministry, is likely to improve their condition and open their minds more thoroughly to the salutary influences of religion and piety; or whether, in a lower degree, the diminution or extinction of that organization through which a thousand nameless benefits find their way to the neediest and most neglected classes of our population, the thousand little acts of occasional help, the thousand acts of charity—whether by the withdrawal of these, disendowment is likely to contribute to the improvement and happiness of the people. God forbid that the established Church of England should stand in the way of the happiness, the improvement, the freedom of mankind. But if, as we are firmly convinced, it is the chief author and maintainer of that freedom, that happiness, and that improvement—if, without the Church among us to give them depth and reality, these benefits would be nothing better than empty names, we are, as a nation, bound to maintain that Church to the best of our ability, and will do so, God being our helper.

CHAPTER VI.

SUPPLEMENTARY.

MEANING OF THE WORD "ESTABLISHED."

THE word *established* is used in so many different senses that unless my readers are careful in distinguishing them it will be impossible to avoid falling into vain and useless discussions. At the hazard, then, of repeating what I have said already, though in a somewhat different form, and reinforcing my previous arguments, I venture to subjoin the following remarks :—

1st. *Establishment*, or *established*, may mean no more than mere existence, with more or less permanency; as when men say they have *established* a club or a library, or a college for working men, meaning no more than that they have set it up and brought it into being.

2nd. It may mean what exists and is generally accepted, as when we say "It is an *established* custom amongst us."

3rd. It may mean that which is legalized or authorized by the Legislature. In this sense every institution or society, or even custom and usage, which has the sanction of the law is *established*, and protected by the law.

But that none of these constitute *establishment* in the disputed meaning of the word is clear; for it is not against *the existence* of the Church of England, nor its *general acceptance*, nor its enjoyment of *legal sanction and protection*, that protest is made. All these things Dissenters enjoy as well as Churchmen. Dissenters in these respects are as much established as the Church of England. In these senses also the disestablished Church of Ireland is established —a condition to which it is sought to reduce the Church of England. So none of these properly constitute establishment.

But objections to establishment are of two kinds.

1st. That it is unjust to the Church of England; and 2nd. That it is unjust to Dissenters.

Neither of these objections apply to establishment in any of the senses mentioned above.

It is unjust, it is said, to the Church, because it brings the Church under such control of the State that it cannot move hand or foot without the consent of the State. It cannot alter or improve its doctrine or discipline, or expand them as occasion may demand. And this restraint is the result of establishment.

It is unjust, it is said, to Dissenters, because

with this slavery the State confers peculiar honours, emoluments, and authority on the Church which it confers on no other religious community.

(*a*) By honours, are meant the seats of the bishops in the House of Lords. But these, as I have shown, are not necessarily the consequence of establishment. The Church would continue to be established even if the bishops were entirely withdrawn from the House of Lords. Thus the exclusion of the majority of the Irish bishops, or the admission of a portion of them into that House after the Union, made no difference whatever as to the *establishment* of the Church of Ireland. These honours, then, do not constitute establishment.

(*b*) By its emoluments are meant the tithes and endowments held by the Church of England. I have shown that these were not given by the State in the first instance, nor transferred from the hands of the Roman Catholics to the Church of England by the State. Therefore they were not established by the State, so far as establishment means either of these things. If it be said that the nation *established* the Church in possession of these endowments, and in that sense the Church is *established*, I reply that if by this expression it be meant that the State put the Church in possession of endowments it had not before, this is untrue, and has no warrant whatever in law or history.

But if it be meant that the State established the right of the Church to its endowments by declaring that right when it was called in question, that is not establishment, nor is it that which is condemned as unjust to Dissenters; for that is what the State does for every one of its subjects, Dissenters as well as Churchmen. A man does not owe his property to the Court of Chancery because in case of a disputed succession it has declared him to be the rightful heir, and established him in possession.[1]

[1] On this point I quote the opinion of an ancient civilian: "Their dueness (i. e. of tithes) being that [which] those statutes did never intend to meddle with, infringe, further, help or hinder, but that they were what they were before. And it were one of the most pitiful pieces of ignorance, befitting only the vulgar herd of unlettered simpletons, and deserving rather commiseration than the exercise of any of our manly passions, to entertain a thought to or toward the contrary.... This is such a shallow conceit as is only worthy the weak brains of the multitude, where only it possibly could be hatched, or can be tolerated or endured; no more excusable than if any should say Aristotle's astronomy gave the sun a being in the firmament; or *Charta de Foresta* first set up game; or a present law, if it should dispose of, did erect parks and chases; or a new order about escheats and mortuaries, the next mistaken age might interpret to give them being and first beginning."—"The Civil Right of Tithes," by E. C., p. 186, ed. 1650.

So, then, the Church's emoluments are no part of its establishment.

(c) By its authority is meant the power of the Ecclesiastical Courts to enforce its decrees. But these decrees, as I have said, so far as they refer to matters strictly ecclesiastical, bind only the members of the Church, and not those who dissent from it; and membership of the Church of England is, at this day, a purely voluntary act, and therefore submission to these decrees must be voluntary also.

Then as none of these things constitute establishment, we fall back upon the fact that establishment is the control of the Church by the State, consequent upon the relations into which the Church was brought with the State at the Reformation, by the establishment of the royal supremacy.

Whatever may have been the inherent right of the Crown—whatever the energy or the effort of various sovereigns from time to time,—this control was never fully established until the reign of Henry VIII[2]. Whatever form that

---

[2] Lawyers and divines at the Reformation contended that this supremacy was the inherent and inalienable right of the Crown; which was no doubt true as a legal maxim. But until the establishment of the supremacy by Henry VIII., it was only true *de jure*, not *de facto*. Of this the reign

control assumes, it takes its origin from the royal supremacy, which became supreme by necessary consequence when the papal supremacy was abolished. So we date establishment, in the strict sense of the word, from the Reformation. In other words, the establishment of the Church, the royal supremacy, the control exercised by the State in all matters connected with the Church of England, are only different expressions for one and the same thing.

In what form that supremacy, or State control, is to be exercised is a mere matter of detail. Whether it be by a vicegerent, or a high commission court, or a court of delegates, or the sovereign in council, it does not touch the principle; that is to say, the supreme jurisdiction of the Crown in all spiritual matters.

Neither is the principle affected by the consideration that in the reign of Henry VIII. there was but one religious society acknowledged by the State, viz. the Church of England,

itself furnishes undeniable proof. The king's divorce was an ecclesiastical cause, which could not be determined by any English court, because it was liable to be over-ruled by an appeal on the part of Katharine to the pope, as supreme. Nothing remained, therefore, for the king except to bow to that supremacy, or abolish it, as he did, and thus make his own courts supreme in all respects, whether spiritual or temporal.

and the Church and the nation were regarded as co-extensive and identical: whereas there are now many religious societies whose existence is tolerated and protected by the law. For, in the first place, the Church of England is still the only recognized Church of the nation, it is the only religious community into which every member of the nation may *claim* admittance, and the claim cannot be denied. And, secondly, every actual member of that Church comes under the same rules and the same polity as were established by the royal supremacy and are still maintained by it. In these respects, and in reference to the Crown, the Church remains in the same essential position as it held under the Tudors—the only difference being, not that the supremacy is altered in relation to those that continue in it, but if the Dissenter will depart, "let him depart."

This being so, it is easy to trace the essential meaning and purpose of establishment by contrasting the authority, freedom, and independence of the Church before the Reformation and after. And as establishment, in its proper meaning, did not exist until the Reformation, it is obvious that whatever honours, power, or riches the Church now enjoys, and did enjoy before the Reformation, cannot correctly be attributed to its establishment, unless we are to suppose that its distinctions and endowments were taken away by Henry VIII. and then restored and augmented by him or his successors—a notion for which there is no foundation whatever in law or in history.

EDITOR'S NOTES.

I.

ESTABLISHMENT.

THERE can be little doubt that Mr. Brewer's view of Establishment is historically unassailable. But although the Church of England cannot be said to have become "established" until the Reformation, so that in considering the act or process of Establishment we must confine our attention to what happened at the Reformation, we shall be very liable to get into confusion if we limit ourselves to this one aspect of the matter. As a rule, when men speak of Establishment, they refer to a *state* rather than an *act*. Now the state of Establishment is not necessarily, or in fact, identical with the act. This becomes obvious directly we consider Disestablishment, which is the undoing of the present established *state* of things, not the mere reversal of the *act* of Establishment. At the Reformation, and for centuries previous to it, the Church had already acquired a certain position and certain powers, not as against other rival religious bodies, but simply as "Holy Church"—the one and only embodiment of the Christian religion recognized. It did not lose this position and these powers at the Reformation, any more than it acquired them. For example, the power of coercive jurisdiction had from an early age been granted to the Church by every Christian State, but not as the prerogative of one out of many religious bodies. There was no competition and therefore there could be no selection. But suppose Disestablishment to happen to-morrow, it would not and could not leave the Church of England just as the Reformation found her. Whatever may be the case with the Church herself, the world outside and the Church's position in the world are entirely changed. She is no longer the sole representative of the Christian religion. There are sects and denominations without end. The sovereign and his subjects may all be Christians—yet one may belong to the Church of England, another to the Church of Rome, a third to the Wesleyan body, and a fourth to the Plymouth Brethren.

A simple undoing of what was done at the Reformation would leave the Church in possession of her ancient coercive jurisdiction; but that would be inconsistent with Disestablishment, as that word is commonly used. To take another illustration. From the earliest antiquity Christian kings have been crowned by a bishop or archbishop of the Christian Church. This practice is, of course, far more ancient than the Reformation Establishment. But if the Church were disestablished, a question would at once arise why should the Archbishop of Canterbury, rather than the President of the Wesleyan Conference, or a Roman Catholic Cardinal perform the rite? Disestablishment would have to deal with this as well as with many other matters which are quite independent of anything that happened at the Reformation. Every one will admit that in such matters as the appointment of Bishops and their connection with the House of Lords, Disestablishment would entail considerable changes in the present external condition of the Church, irrespectively of any historical considerations. Whether we regard these changes as part and parcel of Disestablishment, or as essential accompaniments or precursors of it does not make very much difference theoretically, and practically it is surely convenient to include in our conception of the word as much as possible of what is implied in it. Let us therefore look at the matter under a wider aspect.

Establishment may be described as the national recognition of a particular form of religion, resulting from the relations of the State and the Church towards each other. Our view of these mutual relations must not be restricted by confining our attention to what happened at a particular time, or by particular means. Establishment in any given country is the complex resultant of *all* the mutual dealings between Church and State, since both have existed in that country. It follows that it is not a fixed unalterable thing. It admits of indefinite variety of form. Establishment in Scotland is not the same as Establishment in England. The different Concordats between the European States and Rome are further instances of this variety. Even Establishment in England may be said to have altered from age to age, according to the shifting currents of public opinion, royal policy, and other things. Every resultant must change when the component forces which produce it are changed.

Moreover, as Establishment is to a certain extent a word of varied import, so is Disestablishment, or the undoing of Establishment. It is, as it were, the readjustment of the component forces in such a way that the resultant becomes reversed. A weathercock points east, the wind changes and it points west. These represent the extreme positions of Establishment and Disestablishment, but it is obvious that ,between these two points are an indefinite number of intermediate positions. Thus there are many things which have a tendency to Disestablishment, which alter the direction of the resultant, which give the vane a twist westward, and yet no one of them can be said by itself to produce Disestablishment. Although it seems paradoxical to say so, it may become almost impossible to discern the difference between Establishment and Disestablishment. The weathercock may point so nearly north or south as to make it difficult to decide whether on the whole its inclination is eastwards or westwards. We cannot, therefore, give to this word Establishment, in its broadest sense, any fixed meaning.

All that we can do is to endeavour to set down in order the present features of Establishment, that is the leading particulars of the mutual relations of Church and State in England as they exist to-day. Here again scientific completeness is unattainable. To indicate exhaustively the relations of Church and State would be very much the same

U

thing as writing the History of England. It is obvious that a Church, which for more than eight centuries before the Reformation was the only Christian Church in the land, and which during the three centuries since the Reformation has been the Established or National Church, must occupy, in a great variety of ways, a special relation towards the State, not shared by other religious bodies. What is here sought to be done is to state the principal features of this special relation. In addition to the points enumerated below, there are many minor ties which connect the Church with the State[1].

Disestablishment is the modification of the relations between Church and State in a fundamental manner. The abolition of all relations is a plain impossibility. Every individual, and every society and institution, whether civil or religious, is and must be subject to State control and dependent on State protection. No Church or religious sect could wholly escape from the former, or maintain itself without the aid of the latter. What amount of modification would constitute Disestablishment, it is, as I have pointed out above, very difficult to determine; and by what particular steps Disestablishment, supposing it to occur, would be accomplished is equally hard to predict. Probably the result might be produced in many different ways.

The important point to bear in mind in considering this subject is that Establishment is a complex condition depending on a combination of many different elements. Not every single element, possibly no single element, is essential to

---

[1] Such, for instance, is the sanction given by the law to marriages duly solemnized in church without any civil ceremony. Again, certain personal privileges and immunities still attach to the clerical office, although most of them (e. g. freedom from arrest in going to, and returning from the conduct of public worship) have been extended to Dissenting ministers. Thus clergymen are exempted from paying toll at turnpike gates when on parochial duty.

Establishment. Thus we need not wonder if we find non-established sects in possession of some one or more of the elements of Establishment[2], while on the other hand the Church of England may lose some of the elements of Establishment, and still remain established.

The Mutual Relations of Church and State.

A. *The authority exercised by the State over the Church.*

This authority is the Royal Supremacy, which, as between the Sovereign and the Church, is absolute within its own limited sphere of action, but as between the Sovereign and the State, is controlled by having to be exercised like every other part of the royal power in the methods and with the limitations defined by the Constitution. When we speak of State control of the Church, we mean that the Church is under the supremacy of the Sovereign, and that the Sovereign is subject to the rules of the Constitution. It is in this way that Parliament acquires authority in ecclesiastical matters.

The Royal Supremacy consists of the following particulars:—

1. The Convocations of the clergy cannot be assembled without the King's writ; and no canons can be enacted without the King's licence and assent. Before the Reformation the Crown claimed a certain amount of power over Convocation, but the claim was not very successfully asserted. The royal authority was definitely declared by 25 Henry VIII, ch. 19. The sanction of Parliament is not necessary to the exercise of this part of the Supremacy.

---

[2] An example presents itself in the privilege which at this day probably would be conceded to every religious body to use its own machinery of discipline, in the case of those who voluntarily submit to it; i.e. the exercise of inner or spiritual jurisdiction.

2. The Bishops and Archbishops are nominated by the Crown. This was practically the case before the Reformation, notwithstanding the almost continuous struggle for supremacy, of the Church of England, the King, and the Pope, and the changes which this struggle from time to time produced as one or other of the combatants obtained a momentary advantage [3]. At the Reformation by 25 Henry VIII, ch. 20 (still in force), it was enacted that on a vacancy in a bishopric the King should send to the Dean and Chapter a licence to elect a successor, called a *congé d'elire*, and together with it a letter missive containing the name of the individual recommended by the Crown. The Dean and Chapter are forced to elect the person nominated by the King under the penalties of *præmunire*. In the Crown also are vested the temporalities of the vacant See, so that it can prevent the appointment of any one but its own nominee, by refusing investiture. The sanction of Parliament is not necessary to the exercise of this part of the Supremacy.

3. The Crown is the Visitor of the Church of England [4]. There are traces of a claim to visitatorial power on behalf of the Crown before the Reformation. But so long as the Papal supremacy remained, such a claim could only be vague

---

[3] Stubbs, Hist. Eng. i. 135 ; ii. 316 ; iii. 295, et seq.

[4] "With respect to the nature of a 'Visitor's' duties, it may be laid down generally that they are to control all irregularities in the institution over which he presides, and to decide and give redress in all controversies arising among the members as to the interpretation of their laws and statutes; that in the exercise of these duties he is to be guided by the intentions of the founder, so far as they can be collected from the statutes, or from the design of the institution; that, as to the course of proceeding, he is restrained to no particular forms; and that while he keeps within his jurisdiction, his determinations as 'Visitor' are final and examinable in no other court whatsoever."—Stephen's Commentaries, vol. iii. p. 150. 3 ed. 1863.

and shadowy. At the Reformation by 26 Henry VIII, ch. 1, and later by 1 Eliz. ch. 1, sec. 17, full inherent authority for the "visitation of the ecclesiastical state and persons" was claimed for and declared to be for ever annexed to the Crown. Probably some of the other branches of the supremacy might be treated as illustrations of the visitatorial power, but as they have a clear foundation apart from it by statute, it seems better to deal with them independently.

In fact it is not easy to say what (if any) are the precise steps by which, or the precise purposes for which, the Crown can now exercise its purely visitatorial functions. The machinery indicated by the Reformation statutes and frequently employed by Henry VIII, Edward VI, and Elizabeth was the appointment of Commissions armed with extensive powers. These Commissions were sometimes administrative (e. g. Royal visitations of the Universities and Dioceses) and sometimes judicial. The High Commission Court, which was a Royal Commission appointed for judicial purposes, had a Parliamentary origin, the Crown being authorized to create it by 1 Eliz. ch. 1, sec. 18. Nevertheless, according to Coke[5] the Crown could, apart from the statute, by virtue of its visitatorial power, have erected the High Commission. This particular Court was abolished by 16 Car. I, ch. 11, confirmed by 13 Car. II, ch. 12 and 1 W. & M. ch. 2 (the Bill of Rights). This last Act extended its condemnation to "all Commissions and Courts of like nature." How far these enactments modified or took away the power of the Crown to issue Commissions for judicial purposes has not been decided. That they did not wholly take away the power, appears clear from the fact that Commissions of Review[6],

---

[5] Cawdrey's Case, 5 Coke viii. ix. *Contra* Stillingfleet's Ecc. Cases, vol. ii.

[6] "A commission of Review is a commission sometimes granted in extraordinary cases to revise the sentence of the Court of Delegates, when it is apprehended they have been led into a material error. This Commission the King may

issued by virtue of the Royal authority as Visitor, continued to be granted notwithstanding the Bill of Rights, until their abolition in 1833 by 2 and 3 Will. IV, ch. 92, sec. 3 (the statute which transferred the jurisdiction of the Court of Delegates to the Privy Council). Probably the Crown has still the right to visit by its Commissioners "the ecclesiastical state and persons" for administrative purposes; but here we are without modern precedent, and can only speculate on the present existence of a power, which, except in some extraordinary crisis, is hardly likely to be invoked. The sanction of Parliament is not necessary to the exercise of the Crown's visitatorial authority.

4. An appeal lies in every case from the Ecclesiastical Courts to the Crown. This part of the Supremacy, like those already referred to, cannot be said to have been heard of for the first time at the Reformation. Thus the Constitutions of Clarendon (A.D. 1164) affirm it. But the practice of appeals to Rome prevented the appeal to the Crown from having any real existence until the abolition of the Papal Jurisdiction (24 Henry VIII, ch. 12, and 25 Henry VIII, ch. 19), and the establishment of the Court of Delegates (appeal to the King in Chancery) by the last named statute. The Court of Delegates continued to be the Crown Court of Final Appeal for Ecclesiastical causes from 1534 to 1833, when its jurisdiction was transferred to the Judicial Com-

---

grant, although the Statutes 24 and 25 Henry VIII, before cited, declare the sentence of the Delegates definitive; because the Pope, as supreme head by the Canon Law, used to grant such Commissions of Review; and such authority as the Pope heretofore exerted is now annexed to the Crown by Statutes 26 Henry VIII, ch. 1, and 1 Eliz. ch. 1. But it is not matter of right which the subject may demand, *ex debito justitiæ* but merely a matter of favour, and which, therefore, is often denied."—Blackstone's Commentaries 1st ed. 1768, vol. iii. p. 67. See also Rogers, Ecc. Law, 1840, p. 44 n. and Ecc. Courts, Com. Rep. 1832.

mittee of the Privy Council by 2 & 3 Will. IV, ch. 92, and 3 & 4 Will. IV, ch. 41. The judges in both these tribunals have been the nominees or delegates of the Sovereign. The Crown's jurisdiction is to decide in the last resort every ecclesiastical dispute arising between man and man, which is properly cognizable by the Ecclesiastical Courts, and has been brought before them [7]. This part of the Royal Supremacy has, as we have seen, been regulated by Act of Parliament ever since the Reformation. The inherent power of the Crown as Visitor of the Church to decide ecclesiastical disputes has already been considered. In the case of the Court of Delegates the statute (25 Henry VIII, ch. 19) was held not to oust this inherent power of the Crown exercised by granting Commissions of Review [8]. We may, therefore, without impropriety, distinguish between the visitatorial jurisdiction noticed above and the statutory jurisdiction now under discussion. The latter is in our day of much greater practical importance.

5. No change can be made in the doctrine, ritual, or substance of the Church without the sanction of the Crown, evidenced by an Act of Parliament. The Liturgy, Articles, and formularies, by which the doctrines and ritual of the Church are laid down, are enforced by law, and without a

---

[7] "The scheme is framed on the assumption that every subject of the Crown who feels aggrieved by a decision of any such [i.e. Ecclesiastical] Court, has an indefeasible right to approach the throne itself with a representation that justice has not been done him, and with a claim for the full investigation of his cause. No Ecclesiastical Court can so conclude his suit as to bar this right." Rept. of Ecc. Cts. Com. 1883, p. liii. This jurisdiction in ecclesiastical cases must be carefully distinguished from the spiritual jurisdiction exercised in the Church Courts. The Crown has no power to excommunicate or absolve. It does not claim the "power of the keys," or spiritual jurisdiction as explained *post* pp. 296, 297.

[8] See p. 293, *ante*.

new law they cannot be changed. This part of the Royal Supremacy does not rest on positive enactment, but it is proved by the uniform practice of Church and State since the Reformation[9], and seems essential to any theory of Establishment. How can the State ally itself to a Church without claiming a voice with regard to changes of substance made in the Church? If it were otherwise an Established Episcopal Church might against the will of the State adopt the Presbyterian form of government and yet remain the Established Church.

6. The Crown, with the consent of Parliament, and by means of statutes, has the power of modifying and moulding the machinery by which Church discipline is administered, and the doctrine and ritual of the Church are maintained and protected from infringement. Thus legislation as to the Ecclesiastical Courts has since the Reformation been enacted by Parliament alone, without the sanction of Convocation having been either asked or given. Here again we can refer to no law giving the Crown this right in terms. It rests on the constitutional practice of three centuries.

B. *The principal privileges, enjoyed by the Church, which it is in the power of the State to concede or withhold.*

1. The State (i. e. the Crown and Parliament), concedes to the Church the right to exercise "spiritual jurisdiction" in England. By spiritual jurisdiction is meant, (*a*) enquiry as to the commission of ecclesiastical offences, and (*b*) the pronouncing and annulling of ecclesiastical censures. The power to excommunicate and absolve has always been claimed as a part of the power of the keys given by Christ to the Church and vested in the bishops. Wherever the State has permitted it, the Church has set up tribunals for the exercise of this spiritual jurisdiction. These tribunals are dependent on the sufferance of the State. The power to excommunicate is altogether independent of earthly authority,

---

[9] See p. 211, note.

but the right to use the power in any particular place depends upon the consent of the rulers of that place [1]. This licence to use spiritual jurisdiction has been conceded by the State to the Church of England ever since Saxon times. It is acknowledged in numberless Charters and Laws.

2. The State (i. e. the Crown and Parliament) confers on the Church coercive jurisdiction. Spiritual jurisdiction with its weapon of excommunication is powerless against those who choose to disregard it. It requires to be supplemented by "the civil sword." This the State alone can command. The Church of England has been endowed with coercive jurisdiction certainly ever since the Conquest [2].

3. The sovereign is and always has been from the earliest Christian times crowned by a Bishop or Archbishop [3].

4. The sovereign is required to "join in communion with the Church of England, as by law established," 12 and 13 Will. III, ch. 2, sec. 3; and swears at his coronation to "maintain the laws of God, the true profession of the Gospel, and the Protestant Reformed Religion established by law,

---

[1] See " Necessary erudition of a Christian man " (orders). Bp. Saunderson on Episcopacy, 31, 69 ; Bp. Stillingfleet's Ecc. Cases, ii. 50 ; Sir M. Hale's Rights of the Crown, chap. viii. (MS. in Lincoln's Inn Library).

[2] The fact that the State allows the Church to use its own inherent jurisdiction in its own courts, and enforces that jurisdiction with coercive authority, makes it necessary in the interests of justice that an appeal should lie in the last resort from all Church Courts to the supreme power in the State. Otherwise the State would abdicate one of the first duties of government, that of seeing justice done as between different members of the commonwealth.

[3] "The reader will be interested to know that the Coronation service of the Church and realm of England has been substantially the same from the 8th century to the present time."—Hook's Lives of the Archbishops of Canterbury, vol. i. 341 ; vol. iv. 267.

and to preserve unto the bishops and clergy of this realm, and to the Churches committed to their charge, all such rights and privileges as by law do or shall appertain unto them or any of them." The present form of oath dates from William III's reign (1 Will. III, ch. 6). The most ancient Coronation oath extant (in the Pontifical of Archbishop Egbert, 8th century) refers to the "Church of God."

5. The Archbishops and Bishops have seats in the House of Lords. The Bishops have been members of the Upper House ever since it has existed. They sit as Bishops, and not by virtue of their baronies [4]. The junior Bishop acts as chaplain to the House of Lords [5].

This enumeration of the Church's *privileges*, as distinguished from the points of subordination to the State by virtue of the Royal Supremacy, strongly confirms Mr. Brewer's main position, namely, that the Church became Established

---

[4] Stubbs, Hist. Eng. iii. 430, Hallam's Mid. Ages, iii. 5.

[5] It is a singular fact that the first chaplain of the House of Commons appears to have been a Dissenting minister. The first mention I can find of "Prayers" in the House is the following resolution passed on the 2nd April, 1558, "Agreed upon the motion of Mr. Speaker that the Litany shall be read every day during the Parliament, and a Prayer by Mr. Speaker such a day which he shall think fit at half an hour after eight, and every defaulter to pay four pence to the Poor Box."— (*Hales, on Parliament,* 1707, *London. Professed to be printed from a MS. left by Sir Matthew Hale.*) The clerk of the House appears to have officiated on ordinary occasions. The employment of a minister was first thought of during the Commonwealth. It was resolved on the 13th of January, 1643, "that one of the ministers of the Assembly shall be appointed to pray with this House every morning." 3 Commons Journal, 365. Again, on the 31st Jan., 1658, it was resolved that "Mr. Cooper, who prayed with the House this morning be desired to continue to officiate and perform the duty of prayer in this House every morning during this session of Parliament." 7 Commons Journal, 595.

at the Reformation, and that its Establishment consisted entirely in the control then successfully exerted by the State through the Crown over the Church ; for it will be noticed that, while the State's authority was not consolidated till the Reformation, not one of the privileges referred to above was conferred at the Reformation, they have all been handed down from a far earlier antiquity. Thus, in the sense in which Mr. Brewer has used the word, they have nothing to do with Establishment. Nevertheless, in order to understand the matter practically, it seems desirable, as has already been said, to consider the meaning of Establishment in the wider sense in which it is used throughout these observations. The Royal Supremacy remains even in this extended view of the subject the most important, although not the only feature of Establishment.

L. T. D.

II.

THE "MIXTA PERSONA" THEORY.

This theory, which has probably existed from early times, endows the king in a vague sort of way with some of the powers of the ordained ministry. It is based on the consecration and anointing of the king at his coronation. Lyndwood (lib. iii. tit. 2 § *Ut clericalis:* verb *benificiati*) writes (he died in 1446), "*Rex unctus non sit mere persona laica, sed mixta secundum quosdam.*" It may be inferred from this passage that the alleged dual character was not then universally admitted, although the notion was familiar. There does not seem to be any authority for considering the ecclesiastical supremacy of the sovereign in England as springing out of or referable to any *quasi* clerical endowments conferred on him at his coronation.

The *mixta persona* theory is little noticed (although the expression is used) by English Church writers, either of the Reformation period or later. Hooker's Ecc. Pol. vii. 1 ; viii. 11, 13. Stillingfleet's Ecc. Cases, ii. 121, 124. They defend

the royal supremacy on the ground that God has ordained
kings to *rule* in Church as well as in State, not by the theory
that He has made them *quasi* ecclesiastics with some of the
"powers of the keys." They regard the regal authority and
the priestly authority as both of Divine appointment, but
they do not confound them. The "Divine right" of kings,
of which so much was heard in the seventeenth century, had
reference solely to the rights, powers and privileges of the
"Lord's Anointed" as a temporal ruler. It was wholly
distinct from the "*mixta persona*" theory, and there is
no reason to suppose that those who believed in the former
also held the latter.

Mr. Maskell (*Monumenta Ritualia* iii. xiv) writes, "The
anointing was always held to confer sacredness upon the
person of the sovereign; and for this we have the authority
of St. Augustine, who speaks indeed of the earlier unction
of the Jewish kings; but the argument is the same ' *Quæro
si non habebat Saul sacramenti sanctitatem, quid in eo
David venerabatur ? Si autem habebat innocentiam, quare
innocentem persequebatur ? Nam cum propter sacrosanctum
unctionem, et honoravit vivum et vindicavit occisum; et
quia vel panniculum ex ejus veste præscidit percusso corde
trepidavit. Ecce Saul non habebat innocentiam et tamen
habebat sanctitatem non vitæ suæ (nam hoc sine innocentiâ
nemo potest) sed sacramenti Dei, quod et in malis hominibus
sanctum est.*' The reader will observe that St. Augustine
calls the regal unction, in the above passage, a sacrament:
nor, relying upon his authority, does there appear to be any
objection to the use of so high a term in the same wide sense
in which we speak of the sacrament of orders or of marriage
... But this anointing must not be looked upon, nor ever
has it been, as conferring any sacerdotal right or privilege:
the sovereigns of England are supreme in all cases whether
ecclesiastical or civil, as in the one so in the other, both
before and after the solemnity of the coronation; nor are
their prerogatives increased by its performance or hindered
by its delay." Speaking of the anointing of kings at corona-

tion, Dr. Stubbs (Hist. Eng. i. 146) says: "The ceremony was understood as bestowing the Divine ratification on the election that had preceded it, and as typifying rather than conveying the spiritual gifts for which prayer was made. That it was regarded as conferring any spiritual character or any special ecclesiastical prerogative there is nothing to show: rather from the facility with which crowned kings could be set aside and new ones put in their place without any objection on the part of the bishops the exact contrary may be inferred." It is well to observe this, because nothing could be more fatal to the acceptance, in this day, of the principle of the royal supremacy, than the spread of a notion that it depends for its foundation upon a fanciful theory, probably never generally adopted and now universally discarded. The *mixta persona* theory, in the sense explained above, has nothing to do with the royal supremacy as acknowledged in the Church of England. I do not believe that Mr. Brewer, although (p. 198) he uses the words, intended to convey by them what is certainly their historical meaning. Indeed there is nothing which Mr. Brewer has so conspicuously shewn as that the principle of Establishment is entirely independent, not only of this, but of any other theories, ecclesiastical, constitutional, or other, however eminent the names attached to them, and that it rests on the broad grounds of fact and practical necessity.

L. T. D.

INDEX.

A.

Abbeys, Attractions of, 91.
Advantages of Establishment to Church, 163, 164, 221, 296–298.
    of Establishment to State, 223, 224, 267, 270, 272.
    of Royal over Papal Supremacy, 190–192.
    of Royal Supremacy, 201, 202.
Advowson of Churches retained by Founders, 78.
Aldynge, Vicarage of, 94.
Anglo-Saxons' want of National Unity, 63–71.
Anne's, Queen, Bounty, 109, 122.
Appeals, Statute of, 187, 294.
Appropriations of Tithes, 154, 155.
Augustine, St., on Tithes, 25.

B.

Barrow's, Dr., Benefactions to the Church, 123.
Bishop of Llandaff, Case of, 152.
Bishops did not at first require share of Tithes, 52.
    lived on estates attached to their Sees, 53.
    resigned share of Tithes, 56, 78.
    in the House of Lords, 180, 275, 298.
    Churches built by, 76.
Brinkley, Vicarage of, 95.
Burial in City Churches forbidden, 61.

C.

Chalk, Vicarage of, 96.
Charles I, State of Church under, 108.
Chaucer, Quotation from, 99.
Christianity centred in cities, 27.
    in England before St. Augustine, 33.
    Introduction by St. Augustine, 31–33.
    spread by Persecution and War, 28.
Christchurch, Case of Prior of, 152.
Church and State, Mutual relations of, 291.
    Separate Societies before Reformation, 260.
    Union of, successful, 270.

Church Courts, 181, 283, 294.
Church, The, of England, Benefactions to, 123.
    and Irish Church, Distinction between, 164.
    endowed and under control, 16, 17.
    gives her services, 168, 225, 270.
    Ingratitude of nation, 115.
    Henry VIII gave nothing to, 114-116.
    Edward VI gave nothing to, 119.
    must insist on Creeds, 236.
    not a denomination, 258.
    no common property, 97.
    strength, before Reformation, 186, 296-299.
Churches built by Nobility, 75.
    Chapels of Ease to Cathedral, 76.
    City, Burial in forbidden, 61.
    Gradual growth of, 135, 144.
    Duty of repairing, 143.
    Manorial, and Lay Patronage, 150.
    London and Westminster, 121.
Churchmen only bound by Church Laws, 250.
Clergy, Position of, misunderstood, 268.
Commons, House of, Chaplain to, 298.
    Remonstrance, 100.
Constitution, Establishment vital part of, 11-12.

D.

Danes, Invasion of, 47.
Development, Theory of, 240-243.
    Christian view of, 245.
    does not affect present obligations, 244-247.
Dioceses divided into Parishes, 43.
Disendowment Confiscation, 164.
    Difficulty of, 165.
    unwise as well as unjust, 128.
Disestablishment alone, Effects of, 208, 275.
    destroys Lay control, 226-229.
    implies Disendowment, 165.
    Meaning of, 275, 287, 290.
Dissent, Claims of, 18-20, 207.
    Free and unendowed, 13-16.
Dissenters' liberty more apparent than real, 253.
Dissolution of Monasteries, 104.
Dogma a necessity, 231-234.

INDEX.

E.

Eachard, Archdeacon, 111, 123.
Edward VI gave nothing to the Church, 119.
Elizabeth took First Fruits and Tenths, 120.
Elizabeth's reign, State of benefices in, 108.
Endowments, Church, derived from individual benefactors, 20, 73, 91, 122, 124.
    Church, wisely used, 127, 276, 277.
    Church, robbed at Reformation, 106.
    of Dissenters, 168.
Establishment a complex condition, 290.
    Advantages to Church, 163, 164, 221, 296-298.
    Advantages to State, 223, 224, 267, 270, 272.
    and liberty of the Church, 257.
    brought no wealth or honour, 9, 178-180, 281-283.
    differs in different countries, 289.
    favourable to moderation, 209.
    intended to benefit State, 21.
    Meaning of the word, 182, 279, 280.
    not implied by Endowment, 168, 169.
    not unfavourable to spiritual advancement, 229-230.
    Objections to, answered, 280-281.
    requires fixed forms of faith, 210, 212-215.
    secured a new right to Laity, 258.
    State of, The, 289.
    the control of Church by State, 9, 212, 215, 219, 283.
    Various theories of, 161.
    Vital part of Constitution, 11, 12.
Ethelred, Alleged Law of, 156.
Ethelwolf's grant of Tithes, 53.

F.

First Fruits and Tenths, 120, 121.

G.

Government not wrong in conferring special privileges for national good, 174-178.
Gregory's direction to St. Augustine, 38, 135.
Gunning's, Dr., Benefactions to the Church, 123.

H.

Henry VIII claimed no spiritual function, 188.
    did not create a new Church, 184.

306 INDEX.

Henry VIII did not transfer property to new Church, 173.
    gave nothing to Church, 114-116.
    Letter to Convocation of York, 189.
    's Establishment, 161.
    seized Tithes, 106.
    Statute of Appeals, 187, 294.
Hooker on *Mixta Persona* theory, 198, 200, 299.
    's theory that Church and Nation are one, 205.

K.

Kent, St. Augustine found two Churches in, 33.
King, The, Visitatorial power of, 292.

L.

Laity, Friends of Church among, 266.
    Influence of, good for Clergy, 265.
    Interest of, in Church, 262.
    New right secured by Establishment, 258.
    Usurpations of, 145.
Lay control destroyed by Disestablishment, 226-229.
Lay Patronage of Manorial Churches, 150.
London and Westminster Churches, 121.

M.

Manorial Churches, Lay Patronage of, 150.
Maskell, Mr., on *Mixta Persona* theory, 300.
Mixta Persona theory, 198, 299-301.
Monasteries, Dissolution of, 104.
Monasticism, Revival of, 86.
    Fascinations of, 98.
Monastic and Parochial Clergy, Distinction between, 40.
Monks, Dispersion of, by Danes, 48.
    of St. Augustine laymen, 35.
    Popularity and privileges of, 43-47.

N.

Nobility built Churches, 75.
Norman Conquest, 72, 154.
    Discipline in Church, 80-81.

P.

Parish Churches robbed for Monasteries, 88, 92.
    Tithes settled on, 56, 78, 126.

Parishes derived from Dioceses, 43.
    Gradual growth of, 135–144.
    State of, under Elizabeth, 108.
Parochial Clergy, Anglo-Saxon, married, 44.
    Christianity kept alive by, 49.
    effects of their influence, 82, 85, 113.
    Ignorance of, 44, 71.
    Need for, 44.
    Numbers of, in different counties, 65.
    pauperized by monks, 99.
    pauperized at Reformation, 106.
    promoted in the Church, 51.
    displaced by Edgar, 71.
    in tenth century, 50.
Parsonages, Wretched state of, 111.
Prayer, Common, peculiar to Church of England, 220.
Prayer Book, Changes in, 295.
Property, Danger of interference with, 129–132.
    Individual right to, 11.
    Church possesses no common, 97.
Protection, State, of Church property, 180.

R.

Reformers freed Church from Foreign Jurisdiction, 188.
    made no new Creeds, 188.
    never claimed to create Church, 187.
Reformation, Effect on Church property, 106.
Religious liberty, 238.
Roman art, Remains of, 33.
Royal Supremacy, Advantages of, 201–202.
    Authority exercised over Church, 291–296.
    equivalent to Establishment, 202, 283.
    King's lay character, 198, 299.
    makes Church National, 202–205.
    necessary in some form, 201.
    Objections to, answered, 194–197.
    substituted for Papal, 162.
    what constitutes, 182–183, 291–296.
Rudyer, Speech of Sir B., 108.

S.

Sancroft, Archbishop, Benefactions of, 123.
Selden's view of division of Tithes, 156.

Selden on Origin of Parishes, 78.
Spenser on Robbery of Churches, 103.
Stubbs, Dr., on *Mixta Persona* theory, 300.

T.

Tithes, Appropriations of, 154-155.
  Bishops resigned share of, 56, 78.
  Burial Fees more valuable than, 59.
  Disposition different in different districts, 64.
  Diverted from Parish Churches to Monasteries, 88, 126.
  Duty of payment of, 56.
  Ethelwolf's grant of, 53.
  Present, not grounded on Ethelwolf's grant, 55.
  in the Primitive Church, 23.
  introduced into England by St. Augustine, 153.
  irregularly paid, 57.
  Jewish, 22.
  Monasteries claim, by grant or prescription, 152-154.
  no grant to any special parish discovered, 151.
  not derived from Nation, 9, 10, 126, 167.
  Obligation of, generally admitted as Christianity spread, 42.
  Origin of legal right to, 152-156.
  offered and divided at Mother Church of Diocese, 41, 47.
  Parsons claim, by common right, 152, 155.
  Quadripartite division, 135, 156.
  seized by Henry-VIII, 106.
  settled on Parochial Churches, 56, 78, 126.
  St. Augustine on, 25, 38, 135, 156.
  True history of modern endowments and, 75, 152.
Thorndike, Dr., Benefactions of, 123.

U.

Uniformity of Faith desirable, 236.
Union of Church and State successful, 270.

V.

Vicarages, Institution of, 94-97.
Visitatorial power, The King's, 292.

www.ingramcontent.com/pod-product-compliance
Lightning Source LLC
Chambersburg PA
CBHW030756230426
43667CB00007B/988